JOURNEY
of the HEART

*Transforming the tragedy of a family suicide
into healing, beauty and discovering God*

by Katie Williams

Living Water Publishing
Northridge, California

Journey of the Heart

Transforming the tragedy of a family suicide
into healing, beauty and discovering God

Living Water Publishing
P.O. Box 8419
Northridge, CA 91327
www.livingwaterpub.com

Library of Congress Control Number: 2004096536

ISBN No. 0-9761254-0-4

cover design by Kathryn Marcellino, MarcellinoDesign@aol.com

Contents

—◦◦◦—

Preface

⸻

Just so the reader knows, I did not write this book. That may seem so strange, but I prefer to look at it as God and I wrote this book. I don't know what your religious background is, or what your spiritual beliefs are, but this book is not meant to force anything on you. Quite the contrary, I would like for you to share my journey with me. My 'journey of the heart' which began with me wishing my brother Gabe was in my arms, and ending up with me in God's arms. I would ask that the reader look at what I went through as a mere suggestion or an option, not a request, for how you may handle your grief and loss. This is my journey, and how I discovered lovingly that God was a part of it all along.

Introduction

There are key moments in our life that characterize and help to define all other moments in our life. This book is about one of those moments – when my older brother committed suicide. But before we get into the depth of his pain and his death, I would like to share with you a piece of his life. Gabe was a lively, energetic, fun, 17 year old kid with a zeal for life. Those who knew him best appreciated his humor, enthusiasm, and his ability to make every situation humorous and light. He had that special touch (we all know people like this), that when they step into the room it changes – it gets brighter. He had that kind of shining light, that presence. He was everyone's best friend and he had a way of touching people and making them want to come around him just because of who he was. He was fun, witty, very 'street smart' and could make anyone laugh. I was, and am, proud to call him my big brother. Although we were born eighteen months apart, we were so close and we would share so many private moments together. Our personalities were a compliment to one another. He was mischievous and risky, and I was reserved and followed the rules. We gave each other a piece of ourselves; every once in a while I can still feel myself doing something he would have done, or something he taught me to do.

To help make the picture a little more clear about who Gabe was, and to give a taste of his personality, I would like to share a story with you. I am hoping that this will give you an idea of who he was, and it will make the rest of the book more clear; it will show you more fully who this person is that I am grieving over. Here's the story…

It was late at night and I was about to fall asleep when my bedroom door opened. Gabe walked in, fixing the silver chain on his neck and checking his slightly curly blond hair in the mirror as he walked past it. The baggy oversized jeans he was wearing hung on his legs as he walked over to the side of my bed. His white tank top folded a little on his stomach as he leaned over and said, "Do you wanna take the car out tonight?" He said it with a smile so persuasive he knew he was going to get what he wanted no matter what my initial reaction was. So I agreed and we went out driving around, even though he only had a driver's permit, and he wasn't supposed to be driving without a licensed adult driver. But this didn't bother him much. We drove around the dark streets, looking at all the stores that were closed down for the night. He was relaxed in the driver's seat. His chair was leaned back and he let the wind blow in through his open window. I tried to lean back a little and relax but really I was scared of getting caught, but still excited to be out. I asked him if I could drive too. He told me maybe I could a little later. We must have driven for about fifteen minutes when we saw a police car drive by. Well, that scared us enough to decide that it was time to start heading back home because we considered ourselves lucky to not have gotten caught! I was slightly disappointed though because this meant I wouldn't be able to drive. I knew there was no way he would let me. So he drove us back home and as quietly as we could we returned the car to its parked place, and we crept back into our rooms. His bedroom was upstairs by mom and dad's room, so he had to be extra quiet. My bedroom was downstairs so I didn't have as much of a risk of waking them up. But just the same, we crept to our rooms without a word being spoken.

The next morning at breakfast we gave each other an extra big smile while no one was looking. This was the nature of our relationship; fun, and pushing the limits. For better or for worse, that was Gabe and me.

However, times weren't always so smooth for Gabe and I, or for our family. His energy and tendency to break the rules got him into a lot of trouble. The trouble really started when he was in eighth grade; at least that's when I really noticed it. He was especially disobedient then. I suppose he had a need to break away from everything and assert his independence, or maybe he was just a rebel without a cause. I'm not entirely sure. I still wonder about that sometimes – what was his rebellion motivated by? But I do know that if my parents or his teachers told him to go one way, he would go the other – most of the time. His grades became worse, and he started experimenting with drugs. So he went to a boarding school for two years which was an effort to change this pattern of disregard for rules and authority. When he returned things were good – for a while. But soon the peace at home was broken once again by fighting and struggle between he and our family – mostly with our parents; of course, authority. When Gabe went into high school things got worse than they were before he left for boarding school. It was the same as before: he didn't follow the rules and got into trouble at school, and continued to experiment with drugs and alcohol. He got in trouble for stealing things, and spent a night in juvenile hall – 'kiddy jail'. Later when the problems and the fights and the anger he had inside him got worse, he went to counseling and he got help. But by that time it was so late down the road that his ADHD (Attention Deficit Hyperactivity Disorder) diagnosis and the medicine prescribed to him wasn't very helpful. He continued to do things his way, breaking the rules, and causing our family a lot of heartache. He would do things like run away from home and we wouldn't know where he was or how long he would be gone. But it wasn't all bad, all the time. These hard times were interlaced with great joyous times. Those good times are the memories of Gabe that we, my family and his friends, hold dear and remember the best. We remember the Gabe we love. But to deny this hard time would be to deny a piece of history that existed. To be honest, the last few months of his life are a little hazy for me. I don't remember them so clearly because it wasn't a pleasant time to remember: I just knew my brother was in a lot of trouble, and he told me he felt like a failure. He had lost hope for himself and for his future, and he battled with depression also. At this point I started seeing a side of him that I had never seen before. I started looking at him and not really recognizing him – not that his face had physically changed, but his personality, his moods, and his attitudes did. Gabe would every once in a while, out of anger I think, threaten to kill himself, or say other suicidal things. But we never took him seriously. Later we found out from his friends that he said similar things to them too, but as with most suicidal cases, nobody actually thinks their loved one would actually 'do it'. So the matter is treated lighter than it ought to be. I didn't think he would do it either. It's kind of like winning the lottery – you never think it will happen to you. Not that losing a loved one to suicide is a good thing, not at all. But it's the same feeling of shock. On November 15, 1999 he used a gun to end his life.

Some people may hear that my brother took his own life and they feel deep sadness and sympathy, and they want to reach out and help. However, my view has changed on this topic. It isn't about what happened or didn't happen in the past. I see the issue in a new light now. The night before Gabe died he ran away from home, and didn't tell anyone about his plans. But before he left he cleaned his room and tidied all his shoes and his closet and made his bed with the sheets pulled tight, not even one wrinkle showed. On his bed he left his Bible open with a verse highlighted. It said, "God works all things together for good to them that love God, to them that are called according to His purpose." Romans 8:28. That is really what this book is about. A story of hope and of how God will work everything together for His glory, even through the death of a loved one.

This is really what this book is about. And as you read this journal you may notice words, phrases, and sentences that seem out of the ordinary, or things that are written that don't follow proper grammar rules, etc. In an effort to keep my journal as real and genuine as possible, I have kept some of the mistakes and vague parts in tact, in hope that it will be more authentic and real to you, so you can relate to it. But most importantly, this is a story of hope and of how God will work everything together for good, even through the death of a loved one.

How The Book Came About

OK, I'm listening. I'm listening to what my 10th grade teacher told me – I'm going to write naked. So I'll take off my shoes first, then socks, then jacket... just kidding. Mentally, I must write 'naked' to bear all. And finally I must write one last thing, of how this whole book came together. It started with that time with Laurie at her kitchen table, sipping her iced tea, and me eating cheesecake. Mmmm... cheesecake... anyway, when I told her I wrote about my thoughts, she asked me about them. And we got into deep conversation about the deep complexity of emotions that occur after such a loss. And she said, "You should publish it." The work, the private work, that I had written about Gabe and about the spiritual journey God had led me through as a result of his death. And when she said it, I knew her words were true. So she was watering the seeds that God had planted long ago. Right when she said it, I knew it was true. In an unexplainable way, I felt the Holy Spirit moving in the room, and moving her to say those words, moving me to listen to them. Right after she spoke, she said, "I don't know why I said that, I just felt led to say it." And I knew she was right. I felt the Holy Spirit tugging gently at my heart, waking me up. That was my first introduction to this idea to really publicly share this book with other people. Months down the road, God brought a wonderful Christian woman into my life through the martial arts – her name's Connie. We hit it off right away and I felt a particular closeness with her. He once told me, "God brought us together." And I couldn't agree more. One day, (Tuesday of this week), we got to talking about family and other similar things and she brought up how her brother used to collect antiques. When I asked her about why she used the past tense to refer to him, she told me it was because he had passed away. How? By suicide. I said, "That's how my brother died too!" I couldn't believe we had yet another, so deep, connection! I was excited to discover 'someone else like me,' while at the same time knowing the kind of deep pain she too must have experienced. Now I know so clearly one of the reasons God brought us together – we are so similar and we can help each other! That was Tuesday, today's Thursday. On Wednesday I get an email from Connie saying how she's thought how similar we are, and how she's enjoying our friendship. I had been thinking about the same thing – I wrote her back and told her so. Also in my email box was a note from a close family friend, Don, who I had just gotten in touch with from the last time he and his family were in town visiting my family. Don, like my uncle, is one of the most intelligent, God-like, wise people I know. He is my spiritual role model. And I didn't waste this opportunity to tell him about what has been going on in my life with Connie, and the journal and all of this. Don is also an excellent writer, and he's also an editor. So we'll see where God leads us in that department. Who knows? Maybe Don and I keeping in touch at the right time will lead him to be the editor! We'll see what God does. But before I go on, I must step back to include a very important step.

This morning, and yesterday, I had an itching to show Connie my journal. I have shown it to maybe two people, and I was very hesitant about sharing something so private. But I trust her so much, and I really wanted to share it with her. So I prayed, seeking about whether or not to show it to her. Well, that was clear. I knew after praying that God had definitely given me the OK. It was more than an OK, it was a yes. So I brought the book with me to karate class this morning. All the while I was praying, asking God to please give me some positive reinforcement about what to do with this book. Should I pay attention to what Laurie told me all those months ago? Could this, just my thoughts, actually help people in my situation? So I simply asked God to please give me some positive reinforcement of the publishing idea if it really was something he wanted me to do. At the time, I didn't even know what 'positive reinforcement' meant. I only knew that if He would clearly show me that that was clearly what He wants me to do with this book, then that's what I would do. I simply want to serve Him in as many ways possible, because He is a worthy Leader above all Leaders. And anyone who follows Him closely, I think can also have the potential to be taught by Him to lead like Him.

So anyway, not knowing what to expect, I take the book with me and I say, "Connie, I want to show you something." So I take out the journal, show her a page that I think maybe will give her a feel for the other entries. And I'm just hoping it will give her help or hope in some way. But I really didn't see how my expressed emotions from my situation could apply and assist her with her unique situation with suicide.

And her reaction was absolutely priceless. She reads and intermittently gasps "Ohhhs" and "Ahhhs", and says how it applies to her. Well, that addressed one of my hesitations – and she gave me her truthful opinion. She said she thought it was profound and she loved it.

So I said, "So you really think this could help you?" And in her sweet enthusiastic way said, "Oh yes! I want to read the whole thing! I have chills, I don't know what to say!" And before she finishes reading the entry she says, "You should publish this." Without my leading her to the words they flow out of her. And I knew that God had so clearly answered my prayer. Not only did she give me positive feedback with her response, but she used the exact words I heard from Laurie before. And at that moment, I knew, even more so, that God is amazing. That He answers prayers in the most profound ways. I love Him for that. I love how He loves me, and how He so patiently and clearly reassured me about what I ought to do with this book. He laid it out, clear as day.

I'm still in amazement at how God answered my prayer. Not only did He give me positive reinforcement, but He gave me the exact words I needed to hear. I told Connie a brief version of this story, and I told her that her words were an answered prayer. And I would publish this, in order to help others who know pain like I have known it. But more importantly to offer people the ultimate remedy. The Healer Himself. He allowed pain to come into existence, and He is Love. He created Love and He is Love. His Love is great enough to cancel out the pain. Every time, He never fails. I love His consistency, reliability. I'm sure there will be critics, but I know this is what God wanted me to do. "I can do all things through Christ who strengthens me." *Philippians 4:13*

Romans 8:28

Getting to Know Gabe

It's a long standing tradition in my family to get together with extended family members and friends and go to the Colorado River for a weekend of jet skiing, boat riding, and water skiing. It's a blast to get together with the whole family and have barbeques and bon fires at night. On one of these trips Gabe and I were riding on a jet ski together. Gabe was in the front and I was sitting behind him. Because of his dare devil tendencies he was trying to throw me off into the water! He was driving fast and making sharp turns and seeing how close he could get to skimming the water's surface. He was doing 'donuts', spinning in circles, and we were splashing over the wake of passing boats. He saw a boat headed in the opposite direction and he turned around and headed after it, angling the nose of the jet ski along the curves in the water so he could jump the wake and 'get air' as he would say. With his speed and daring sharp turns, I was hanging onto his life jacket for dear life! I didn't want to fall off because I knew it was exactly what he wanted, and it would only give him a good laugh at me! So I was trying my best to hold on tight, and we exchanged laughs because we both knew he would try to throw us off; his preference would be that only I fall off!

And he succeeded – with one whip and unexpected turn I fell off the back of the jet ski and landed half way in the water with my legs still on top of the water craft. It happened rather quickly, but he fell backward too, and landed on top of me, crushing my knee between his body weight and the machine. He was laughing when we fell off, but when he saw that I was hurt, his laugh faded – that laugh that people say we shared. My friend once called it, "The Williams' family laugh". My uncle saw that we were in the water and came over to see if we were all right. He pulled his jet ski next to ours and turned it off and jumped in the water. He was looking at my legs to make sure no serious damage was done. I wasn't seriously hurt, but I did want to go back to the house to rest for a little while. So Gabe and I crawled back onto the seat and we started driving back to the dock. On our way back I told him he better drive me straight back in, and not try any more turns that might get us thrown off again! Being the typical jokester that he was, he make a quick move of the handle bars, suggesting that he might try to make another fast move and land us in the water again! He was laughing, and turned his head around to see if he had gotten to me. I was trying to keep my straight face to show him that I was serious about not wanting to fall off again, but I laughed too. He was always one to joke around and try to get a rise out of his victims! For the rest of that river trip I would not ride with him, even though he promised he wouldn't make us fall off again. I knew him better than that than to fall for it!

Gabe was leaving home on bad terms and I didn't know when he would be back again. All I knew that morning was that he was going to stay with his friend, a person I had never met. He was going to an unknown location for an unknown amount of time. His friend circled about half way down our street to pick him up, and Gabe was clutching the straps of his duffel bag. Jake and I walked our older brother down the street to see him off. I looked at him walk toward the car and watched him as he put his bag in the back seat and close the door. I was looking at him about to leave me, how dare he, and I didn't know what to do or say. So I stood in my bare feet staring at him. He was talking to Jake, and I was scared and angry at the situation. I wanted to reach out and grab him, make him stay at home, but I couldn't change his mind. I turned around so he couldn't see the moisture gathering in my eyes. I wanted to be strong for him and for myself, and I wanted to show him that I wasn't scared, that I believed I would see him again soon. But the truth was I didn't know when I would see him again, and I was scared. Jake and Gabe had finished saying good-bye and I turned and faced him. I didn't care if I started to cry, I had to say good-bye to him even if it meant I had to let my guard down against him. I had no words for him, and he had none for me. His facial expression mirrored my own, and he was just as scared as I was about him leaving home, not knowing what awaited him. I grabbed him and we hugged each other tight and started to cry. Suddenly the walls had been knocked down, and we both showed our fear through those tears. He grabbed the fabric of my jacket and gripped it tight, closing his fingers into a strong fist as we buried our heads into one another. The embrace didn't last very long, and when we parted we put our game faces back on. That was when he promised he would call soon. It was one of those lifechanging moments that remains vividly in my mind. Jake was looking on at us, and Gabe's friend waited patiently in the car. And with that, he got into the front seat and was carried away by that little brown car. Jake and I walked back toward home silently.

This is a story that I didn't like to think about after he died. We were treading water not far from where the houseboat was docked on Lake Mead. Gabe and I had been going at it, fighting about something that wasn't very important. We were yelling at each other, tormenting, and teasing each other in an effort to push each other's buttons, seeing which button created the most reaction. Whoever could get the other more angry or frustrated won the battle. Being on a houseboat with him for a few days, in close quarters, only acted as a catalyst for our irritation toward one another. The two of us were swimming with our cousins and siblings, continuing to bother one another, and one thing led to another and we started fighting again. The splashing turned into hitting, and I grabbed him and put him into a chokehold. Bad idea. I held him tight, all the while we were both treading water underneath us. I held him there for a little too long. I released him and pushed him away from me, fighting the resistance of the water as I put distance between us. He squirmed out of my released grip and turned and looked at me with so much anger, and his face was very red. He was so angry that I think he scared himself and me, because he didn't charge after me again to take the upper hand and outdo me. He swam away yelling profanities and words that made mom upset with both of us. My heart felt heavy with guilt because I knew that line of proper behavior had just been crossed. After that we didn't talk for a little while. Gabe didn't come near me, and I didn't go near him. We had our ups and downs.

Journal Entries

❦ *November 16, 2000* ❦

I'm not exactly sure why I'm writing this. I suppose it's just a way to remember everything – a way to look back and recall the events that have taken place. Yesterday was weird. I never expected it to come back on so strong. It was feeling it all over again in some ways – yet so different in other ways. Last year it was a lot stronger, more intense. I felt it every second of every day. I tried hard to continue on with everything: school, karate, everything. I tried to speed everything up, keep myself busy, avoid pain. This year I wished I could have slowed it down. I was thinking about HW and other stuff – mostly just schoolwork – but it was so hard to concentrate. I wanted so much to not feel it at all; yet I also felt my heart crying out so loud. I never knew how much I missed him. I mean I did, but I don't want to think about it a lot – it slows me down, stops me from finishing everything that feels so urgent at that moment. Do people think I avoid it? Maybe. I know some do – I don't care. We all take it in our own ways. I could write about this forever. There's no end to it – there never will be. The seas will calm but the storm never ends; not until the Father chooses that end; the end of my life. Until that point it continues. It's always with me. Even though I don't dwell on it all the time, its there. I'm not sure if I think about it every day – I probably do. Whether it's for a split second or for a minute. Either way it's always in the subconscious mind. I feel like I hardly know him – it's been so long that we've last spoken, and it's hard to remember things. I'm sad because I know that as time passes I lose memories. I know that there will always be a select few that are forever a piece of my heart and my soul even (if that's possible). I prayed about a few of those memories last year – I prayed I wouldn't forget them – and I haven't. That is a blessing, I am sure. Whenever I'm down I think of those few things and how much they meant to me at that time, and even more so now. How did this ever happen? Why didn't I see it? And even on that exact day, I told the cops at my door that I didn't think he was serious – I didn't. Who did? Who didn't see this as a surprise? Not a soul. But nevertheless, I still know that God's in control. That's all that matters. "Draw near to Him and he will draw near to you." So true. A lesson I learned well and I'm still learning. After all, the whole learning process is always continuous, right? I remember praying and just faintly feeling God. Like I knew he was there, but he wasn't responding to me. He gave me no feedback. It only frustrated me more. But when He doesn't offer answers, He offers Himself. That's another important lesson I learned. Although I never had words to put to it later. When I heard those words, it had then made sense what had happened during that prayer. Will anyone ever read this? I doubt it – I won't ever show anyone. A lot of good has come from it, but is that the only way it could have been attained? What would it be like of he were here now? Weird! In the first year all I could think about was how unreal it all was – how he's on vacation or something. Did I really believe that, or was the other option too scary to accept? I think I really did think he was just gone for a while. It couldn't be true. Why was everyone so sad? Didn't they know it was all just a joke? He'd be back – why was their faith so small? Or maybe they were all wiser than I, ready to face the facts. Either way, I knew it was real at the funeral. It's as if I could deny it, turn my face from it – until I saw him (casket). There was no more denying it. We walked down the isle, casket leading, my right arm hooked with my dads – I could not hold strong anymore. I remember putting my head on my dad's shoulder as if he would hold me up. I heard the Mariah Carey "One Sweet Day" and I questioned if I would be able to even hold myself – I felt so weak inside. It was November 20, 1999, five days after. I remember not looking anywhere but straight when we walked down the isle. I didn't want to see anyone's faces. I didn't want to know who was watching me like this. I don't know why but I just don't want everyone seeing me cry. I feel weird. People don't know what to do and neither do I. The slide show was good – when I saw the pictures I was smiling, remembering the good times. Everyone else was crying. I remember hearing the sobs echo throughout the sanctuary when the song ended. Then I suddenly remembered where I was. Seeing his good friends made me hurt – especially Trevor. I'm not sure why. Maybe because their relationship was so exclusive – just the two of them. I'm tired. I'll write more later.

❧ November 29, 2000 ☙

OK, I obviously had a lot of stuff going on in my head that day. I don't get it. Sometimes it's fine, other times, it feels as if it takes my all to control it for a split second. To hold back a tear, push away a thought… all done in effort to keep my composure – usually not that, though. Usually to keep myself on my work, or whatever task it is. Usually it's because I want so much to continue with the present activity that it doesn't matter what else I'm feeling. Sometimes it's just a roadblock to me. I want to keep going, but it holds me back, usually just mentally. Most of what I do involves a lot of mental concentration, and when I'm thinking about everything else, I can't put all my effort into what I really want to be doing. It's like a memory: when you wish it would go away it only lingers, torturing you more. But when you try to recapture a memory they flee like the darkness when you flood a room with light.

❧ *December 9, 2000* ❧

I thought about him a little bit today. It was the Black Belt test and it was the presentation on belts. Mr. Fox said how Danielle's Dad died and it reminded me of just six months ago when Gabe got an honorary belt, and Jake and I were crying. It was the same kind of thing but only I saw Diane and Danielle sad. Actually Danielle kept it together. It was all those same emotions again.

This week Hillary told me that she cried when I did on my test in June. I thought it was kind of cool. People don't ask much about it anymore. Jess wrote me a letter on the subject and just how she didn't ask me how I was doing and stuff, and it touched me so much. I cried so hard. I feel so close to her and because she knew Gabe well (because of Kim, Michele and friends) it makes it mean even more. I can't believe it's been over a year. I can still hear his voice, his laughter. I can picture perfectly all his mannerisms; but yet I still feel like I don't even know him. Just like when you don't keep in touch with a friend you aren't as close anymore. You don't talk to them anymore. That's how this is. That's why I feel like I don't know him – I haven't talked to him in so long that I feel I'm not as close to him anymore. In the beginning I thought he was going to come home. I wanted him to – I expected it. But now I don't wish he was back because everything would be too different.

❧ *December 11, 2000* ❧

Christmas is near. I remember this time last year. I kind of secluded myself when people would ask me questions. I would only talk to the people I wanted, when I wanted. It was as if I was storing it all up until one day it would all come flowing out – when I thought it was safe. As with all private or secluded things, they usually occur at night – no one's watching; it's a safe time. For me everything all came out at night when I let it. Although sometimes it flowed out at the least expected time – and usually right when I didn't want it to. Even though my mind was so focused (or I was trying to focus it) like at karate, it would still pop up into my head. I don't know. So now even to this day, at night time all my emotions come out. Often I don't mean for them to come out like that. They just do for no apparent reason. Nothing triggers it. It just starts to flow as if on its own, with a mind of its own.

❦ *January 4, 2000* ❦

Christmas wasn't too bad. I only felt it more toward the end and after x-mas. I think it takes some time to let it all sink in – what this all really is – the second Christmas. I always wait till after – I don't know if it's by instinct or what, but I do. I think I do that because everyone's gone, cleared out. Everything's over then I can slow down. I've really been feeling it lately. The first few months it was all about him – when is he coming back, why didn't he care, I wish he were here... After that its all about me – how am I going to go on, how is my life going to be now, I'm so sad, I can't do this or that, when is this pain going to stop because it hurts me... Now its both – it's where is he, but it's also, how am I going to deal? Why do I feel it so much now? It's been over a year. It never feels this strong throughout the rest of the year. I think it's because the break gives you time to think and reevaluate everything. That's probably why it comes up now. I remember one time I was trying to talk to Trevor outside of the house and I could barely get one word out – if I tried to say anything it would just come out as tears. I did talk. I tried so hard but I couldn't hold back tears no matter what. But that was a long time ago. I would never be that out of control now. It comes up a lot at karate. Since I was there when it happened, that's probably why I get so emotional at karate sometimes. Not really, but I don't show it. Sometimes in that parking lot when I'm alone – I just think a lot. I think it's more about him and not me. I've learned to live with it – so it's not about 'what will I do' anymore. Now it's more about him... I miss him, wish he were here, wish I could have used my time better; talk to him, anything. Just to make me more at peace now. Until later...

❧ *January 17, 2001* ❧

OK, I don't get it. I wasn't even thinking about him like at all today, but for whatever reason I'm thinking about it now. Maybe because Jake said, "Remember when Gabe…" something. I forgot what he said. I don't know. It's just like a sadness that comes over me, sometimes for no reason, like today, and I just recognize it when I feel it. And when I do feel it, I try to convince myself that the pain is from something else – some other emotional thing going on within me. That pain is easier to deal with than the pain of what it really is. Well, I'm used to it. Sometimes I smile on the things we used to do, or the things he used to do, but that's about it. I'm used to how my life is. Although at times it does feel like I'm lacking somewhere. I've gotten more and more accustomed to that missing "thing". I'm a better person because of this struggle, and a prayer fixes everything. It transforms me, makes everything OK again and gets my head on straight. At least I can smile at it now. It's good to be able to do that and not worry about what the future holds. I'll get there one step at a time.

❦ *April 9, 2001* ❧

I think being alone triggers it the most. Something about being alone that allows your thoughts to flow freely. It's a mental choice, really. You can decide what you want, and I think naturally your body will lean toward that. I went to the gravesite on Sunday, (4/8/01), for the first time in a long time. I think I don't cry when I'm there, though, hardly ever. It may draw a tear or two, but it's when I get back into the car that I'm really feeling it. Again, it's something to do with being alone with your feelings. I feel safer that way – no one to look on, no one to judge, just me, my thoughts, my tears, and my Comforter. He's the best. The only One who's always there. He knows everything and just how to comfort me. Too bad I have so much trouble communicating this to others. I'll figure it out sometime... I thought I didn't care that much anymore. This time the tears weren't so much about him, or missing him. They were more about how touching it was of the people who tried to help him. As I was leaving the cemetery (Oakwood Memorial Park), I thought I saw Dan Fera drive by in his car. That made me cry harder. Thinking of their hospitality and how much they did for him over his lifetime. They're such great people who loved him a lot. I also think about Dean from church. How he used to ask me about Gabe, how he told me he paged him, tried to contact him, talk to him. Each time he asked me about my bro, I could tell how much He really cared – it was all written in his eyes. The eyes are the windows to the soul. Then I think about how hard it used to be, and how much I've changed since then, for the better, yes. But would there have been some other way? A way that could have been accomplished without him dying? But how much worse off would our family have been if he were here? Unanswered questions. But then again, if he hadn't have died, how would I ever have become so close to Josh? I wouldn't have, and that alone is a blessing that makes his death more easy for me to accept. Do I really miss him? Yes. But I think a large part of that is sadness and curiosity about what life would have been if he were here. That is a huge meaning behind the words, "I miss him." Got to go to karate now.

Gabe and Katie ages 17 and 15, at a friend's birthday party

❧ *April 15, 2001* ❧

I feel moved to write. I'm not sure why. It's Easter
Sunday and Josh and his family will be over at 2:00 for a bar-
becue. It makes me think of Gabe just because it's Easter.
Whenever I get close to God, I think of Gabe. How could I
not? When I'm speaking with the Commander of heavens
armies, how could I not think of one in heaven? I always
think of my brother when I'm speaking to his Caretaker.
Whenever something goes wrong, I find a way to relate it to
Gabe. Either I think of how it would be different if he were
here, and maybe there would be no problem; or I think of any
tears as sad tears. And if I cry about this problem, I'm suddenly crying about Gabe, the problem at hand, that issue that
was bothering me last week... and it goes on and on. And if
something really good happens, and I quietly say a little
prayer of thanks, I think of him then, too but in more of an
endearing, loving way. And I feel both a connection with him,
and an even closer connection to God because it was through
Gabe that I became so much closer to Him, and He under-
stands everything. He knows all the feelings that are brought
about by it. When I talk to God, I feel I'm speaking with
someone that's abounding in love, and I also feel His wisdom
and His knowledge of me as a person, as well as my life and
the future He already has planned and knows about. I feel that
when I talk to Him. That He knows all of my past, He was
there with me through it, even when I didn't realize. And I
love knowing that He already knows my future and He's
there. He knows the steps I need to take to get where He
wants me to go – and He's here to lead me to those steps.
He's there at times to walk in front of me to lead the way,
sometimes behind so I'll venture out, take a leap of faith, and
give it a try on my own – but He's still there. Sometimes He's
there to walk beside me, just to walk. Just to be there for
whatever may come – because sometimes the road I travel

isn't full of twists and turns, roads and roadblocks. Sometimes the walk is just casual, but He's my Companion for that, too. Sometimes it's hard then He carries me. But that's seldom. Usually I just need a little guidance, so He takes me by the hand and gently leads me through. Anyway, I don't know why, but I just thought I'd write that. Everything is OK in the end; if it's not OK, it's not the end.

Gabe 4 years old, Katie 3 years old, getting dressed up

❧ May 17, 2001 ❧

"Sometimes I still feel you" was the name of the song. I wish I could remember the rest of the words. It was strange. Brought back a lot of old (well, not that old, I guess) feelings. I want to use this pen so I can see how it looks when I write with it. It looks cool. I like it. Anyway, weird how things can bring back a memory. OK, I just like writing with this pen. I don't really think about it much, but sometimes it just hits you. What's in the subconscious areas of your mind travels to the conscious area sometimes.

❧ May 22, 2001 ❧

I remember in Algebra II class last year, Mr. Kwong's class, I was sitting in the back of the room, the last chair in the center row, (the class was so full), and for whatever reason I felt it. I put my head down on my folder, as if I were going to sleep and I cried silent tears, watched them as they dripped to my folder.

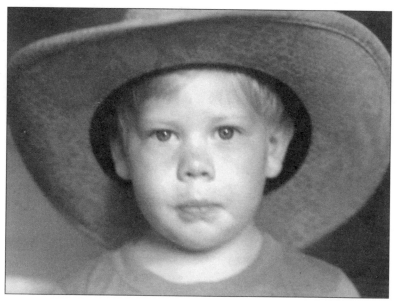

Gabe at age 6

❦ May 23, 2001 ❧

I think that the human mind, body (well, maybe not body) can overcome anything. No matter what the case is. If given enough time, I am confident that all can be overcome. Perhaps it is because our memory is busy storing other things, and consequently disregards what was once held so high in importance. Or perhaps it's because we don't want to remember what it was, so we put it off into the back of our minds, and eventually it fades softly away in the backdrop, the actors on stage unaware of it all the while. And then where does it go? If no one is aware of it, is it still there? Or does it become merely a chapter in the book of life?

✄ June 7, 2001 ✄

I had a dream. I saw him last night. It was weird but kind of cool too. He seemed really relaxed, cool. He seemed so controlled, and like he had it all together. We were at a family wedding, I dreamt, and we had all arrived. We were by the parking lot, as if waiting to go inside. Then he pulled up. He was in an old grandma-looking type of car. Very strange. He wasn't much taller than me. I was kind of surprised he was there, like I wasn't expecting to see him. I asked him what he was driving, and I forgot what he told me, but it was basically a non-informative answer. He told me I couldn't drive it. That answer surprised me a little, but I wasn't angry. When we were standing side by side, he have me a little hug, like a, one arm over the shoulder type of hug. He's never done that before as far as I can remember. Then he told me I looked like such a woman. (Or I was turning into one or something like that.) The kind of thing you hear from realities at a family reunion or something. And this was like a family reunion. I haven't seen him in a long time. It was like he was saying it in a tone and a manner that showed he hadn't seen me in a long time. It touched me. I can't put into words exactly what I felt by his touch and by his words. Like being reunited with an old friend that you've been waiting to see for so long. I felt special that he was talking to me before the rest of the family. I felt important to him, like he picked me. He was talking to me, and wasn't in a rush to go anywhere. Wasn't in a rush to talk to anyone else that was at the wedding. If only I could express the grace and the compassion I felt when he put his arm around me and when he spoke to me. It's like when you talk to an old friend. You can tell them the same story you told a hundred people, but it means more when you tell them because they know you're whole past. So it somehow makes the present story more meaningful. The dream was so short, but it touched me so much. I felt as if he were visiting me or something. Like he was dropping in to see how I was doing; see how things were going, spend some time and comment on how I had changed. It made me realize how much I miss him. How much he means to me. I was reminded of that when I felt a bit of his personality. I told Sara about my dream. I told her who I saw, but I didn't tell her all the details yet because we were on the phone. Well, the bell is going to ring soon...

**Gabe at age 17, Katie at age 15, the night of Homecoming;
one of the last pictures taken of them together**

⊱ July 12, 2001 ⊰

I've had so many dreams lately. Gosh, I miss him so much. The house was so empty today... it felt lonely, I felt lonely. I thought that maybe if he were here, maybe the house wouldn't be so empty, quiet: Zack in summer school, Jake at boot camp, mom on an appointment, dad at work early – not the ordinary. Why was it so quiet and why was I thinking about him? I told Josh I felt lonely. He asked why and I told him because the house was quiet. But I didn't really tell him why because I didn't want to say it out loud. It makes sense in my head, but not out loud.

The first dream was on the previous page.

The second was about a week ago or something...
We were all at a sleepover, a bunch of my friends, mostly girls, like thirty, and everyone was talking about the same thing... "Gabe is back from heaven..." I don't remember much more than that. Only that I was so happy. My heart burst with joy. I was so excited that he was back; he was home. I was so excited that I was crying in my dream – or so I thought. But my tears were real. I woke up crying out of excitement, love, joy, pain, happiness; hope that it was all over. But I awoke crying even harder, realizing that it was a dream. I was so sad – more than I was happy when "he was back." I was sadder because it was a crash. Right in the instance before I awoke, I could feel myself waking up, and I thought, " I'll know it's true if I wake up and he's here." But I awoke only to myself, and my hopeful tears, wanting my dream to be true. The disappointment of my life, probably. Oh, I was so excited that he was home. I really believed it. I wanted to believe it. But back to my dream... everyone was leaving my house from the sleepover... they were going home. And I was standing in the doorway, saying bye as they all filed out, single file in a line. And as he passed me I gave him a big hug. We both hugged each other, so happy to be

reunited. I wanted it to be true. Why do I have to live without him, only seeing him in my dreams?

Sara had a dream that Gabe came down from the sky in a white light, telling us we shouldn't be thinking about heaven. Telling us that, "It took me a long time to get these," (wings) but that our life was on earth now, and not to think about our life in heaven. Our life was on earth right now. He was dressed like an angel, Sara told me. She called me crying, just waking up and remembering her dream. I was really touched by it. You never know just how much something means when you do it. But to the receiver, it means the world. I'm tired now. Bed now, write later.

❧ *August 26, 2001* ❧

I'm thinking of him so much more lately. Maybe it's
because I'm going to be a Senior, a step he never got to. So
once again, this incident long ago affects me another way
today. It's like crossing a long, long bridge. Sure, you've
stepped on many different boards while crossing, but there
are many new boards ahead, each a different color, size,
shape. Each that your foot will fit to differently. Although I
used to think the only struggle I had was to deal with him not
being here anymore – I am wrong. That struggle is only one
board I pass on my way across the bridge. There are many,
many ahead that I've yet to face. I think that's the way it's
affecting me now is not losing him, but coming to the realization that I'm surpassing him and his life steps. Like
school, he was never a Senior, but now I am. He never gradu-
ated, but now I will. He'll never go to college, get married, or
own his own business. He will never have children, stroll on
his back lawn, holding a drink maybe, loosen his tie after a
long hard good money-making day at work, and gaze at the
moon. He'll never do that. I'm sure he's got a great view of
the moon – if he wanted it. But how do you compare the
beauty and serenity of paradise to a dirty window view of paradise? No comparison. Why buy a lemon air freshener when
you can dwell in the grove where the idea for the freshener
was imagined? So why would he care to look at the moon
now, when he has a view far superior any time he wishes to
enjoy it? Exactly my point. He wouldn't even care to look at
the moon now.

✎ *August 28, 2001* ✎

I just finished reading a book today, *Joni's Story*, which is a story of a Christian woman who was paralyzed in a diving accident and now has a ministry dealing with preaching to the handicapped. And she travels all over the world, telling her story and how God worked in her life.

In her book she wrote that she could feel that God was preparing her for something. Those words touched me strongly because I have also been feeling very similar things. Like I know something BIG is coming up in my life. Very big. And I'm not expecting it tomorrow, next month, or even next year. Only that I know I'm going to be doing things drastically different than I'm doing now. Joni wrote that she felt God was preparing her for something – that's kind of how I feel.

Lately I've been praying for direction, like what to do next, and each time I do, something comes up. I've been praying about ways to make good money. My parents do and I just hope that I'll be able to do as well as they have, and give my kids as much as they have given me. And there's no career that I'm really excited about going in to. The only things that are exciting to me are movies (movie-making) and the White House, and the Presidency in general. So anyway when I was thinking about my financial future, and praying about it, the company MCT got brought up. This was about a week afterward. I went to Russ's house for a presentation with Josh, and I thought, "Wow." It sounded really good. And for two days after, it's all I was thinking about. It just sounds so right and right when I was praying about these things. The MCT meeting was on Sunday, now it's Tuesday, and I was thinking and talking about it on Sunday, Monday, and a little today. It was on my mind and heart. It just seems like the opportunity God is bringing. I keep thinking about how I would do it, how I would make it work. Maybe this is a part of what's coming up. But I think it's more than that too.

✖ *March 18, 2002* ✖

It's been a long time since I've written. Sometimes I have so much emotion. I'm not sure where it comes from. Like I'll be so happy and excited and looking forward to something one moment, and the next I'm no longer thinking about the excited thoughts. Now I'm thinking about something sad. It's like the sad emotions are deeper and can more easily sweep away the good thoughts out of mind. Isn't it strange how we can put a huge issue out of mind? Like by a simple exercise our mind can be completely transformed and fixed on the matter that is at hand. That's why exercise and working out can be such a blessing. Ok, what am I talking about? Anyways, I can remember talking to a friend's uncle who was going to become a psychologist, and he said girls and guys couldn't be best friends. He said it was impossible because eventually one will end up liking the other, or the feeling is mutual. So his idea is that it's impossible for a guy and a girl to be best friends. I suppose that's right, but then again, what fun would it be if you could never play love games and have the excitement of liking someone then finding out they feel the same. I suppose it all starts with friendship. Anyways, this was a weird entry. I didn't really go with it where I wanted to go. Until next time…

❧ *March 19, 2002* ❧

Now I think I have more clarity than I did last night. What really was on my mind was college. I feel like I limited myself by listening to my parents and doing what they told me to do: go to a junior college, transfer from there. Now I don't know how to think about the issue. There are two main thoughts/standpoints I have on it. First, if I do stay at home, I could save money because I wouldn't be paying rent or high tuition prices. I could figure out what I want to do, get my general education out of the way, then transfer after the first two years. Sounds pretty smart right? Well, maybe I don't want the smart choice. Maybe I don't want the map; I'd rather stumble and fall than be given all the answers. At least if I was making a mistake by going away to college, I'd be making my own mistake, and not getting all the answers right simply because someone told me they're right. Who cares about doing the "right" thing? Who says it right? By whose standard is this measured? Why should I listen to my parents, go to a junior college, and do what they say is "right", or the "best decision". I want to find my own definition of "right", my standard of evaluation, not theirs. If that means I go away to college and make mistakes, waste money, so be it. At least I'm discovering it for myself, rather than take their word on everything. I'd rather get the heck out of here, go away to college, and have my own experiences, discover things for myself – No more road maps.

I'm a lot less emotional tonight because I already got it all out on the phone last night to Josh. I was going crazy on the phone, getting so mad at myself for listening to my parents, like I always do. And this is the first time that I so bitterly regret following their advice, or rather, instructions. I should have done what I wanted to do. I should have applied to a few schools, maybe I would have gotten in, and I'd be a lot more satisfied right now. But instead I'm going to sit at home for the next two years as my friends go away to college, and I'll wonder, "What if...?" The reason it's so painful to accept is because I'll never know. Maybe I could have been in a whole new atmosphere, meeting new people, experiencing new things at a new college in just a few months. But I won't know because I followed what my parents told me and limited myself. Forget the money. Who cares if it's the "smarter" thing to do? It's not what I want! I want to go away, to become more independent, to find out what I want out of life on my own; no more advisors, no more babysitters. If I stumble along the trail, fine. At least I'm walking without a leash on. I'd rather figure out what I'm going and where I want to go in life out there, out in the real world, not sitting at home with my same lifestyle going to this junior college garbage. Why was I so dumb to let someone else make such an important decision for me? OK, so my parents have the money and they say junior college. But realistically I know that if I went ahead and applied somewhere they would end up paying for it. So frustrating! Why did I work so hard for good grades in high school then? Ugggh! I'm an idiot for not listening to myself and what I really wanted for me. They're not going to live my life for me, so why should I make judgments based on what they believe? Anyways, it's getting late now...

❧ *March 20, 2002* ❧

Somehow even though you don't think anyone is watching, someone always is. Why is that? I don't know. Last month I was so worried about my future. Where was I going to go? What was I going to do? The question every older adult likes to ask is related to college plans, career goals. "What are you going to major in?" they all ask. But now there seems to be more clarity. Today my philosophy teacher said to me, "You're going to make a great attorney one day." I thought yeah! That solidifies my decision because if someone who doesn't even know me that well can see qualities in me that are useful in law, then I feel like that's where I should be. I first realized I wanted to go into law when I was reading the article on Andrea Yates and I realized: had her prosecutors not been as good as they were, this woman could have walked free, never being punished for the crime of drowning her 5 children. I was reading it, and it hit me in the heart. This is what I need to do. I need to make sure that women like this can't walk the streets free after such a crime. I can't believe I didn't see it sooner. I can easily envision myself as a lawyer, or maybe a businesswoman, possibly both. What's amazing to me is how last month I was lost, and today I can see the light up ahead. Amazing what prayer can do. Honestly, I haven't figured out why God is so good to me. Whenever I ask for something, He always gives it to me. Why? I'm a sinner like every other. I'm astonished that He is so faithful while I struggle to keep His commandments. I'm so glad that He's here, though. Although I don't know the way, my Tour Guide does, and that's all I need.

❧ *April 9, 2002* ❧

Yesterday I was thinking... he's supposed to be here. He's supposed to be turning twenty... next month, Josh reminded me. I wonder what he would have looked like, what he would be doing. Would he be at community college, or maybe working? And if he were working, what would he be doing? Would he be bothering me, or causing the family trouble? Are we better off this way?

❧ *April 10, 2002* ❧

I can still feel him. People used to tell me, "He's not gone." I didn't believe them. He's not here. I don't see him, don't feel him. Can't hear him. He's gone. They're just saying that because it sounds good, right out of a Hallmark card. He's not here and they're trying to feed me B.S. that sounds good and sentimental, but no one really believes it. Now I believe it. Of course he's here. I can feel him in my heart, hear him in my laughter. Sometimes I even hear his words when I speak. That's what happens when you spend your whole life with someone. He's an integral part of me. Just because I can't reach out and touch his face doesn't mean it's not real in my mind. I can see him perfectly. OF COURSE HE'S HERE! I realized it today. He's taught me so much and influenced my life and way of thinking greatly. He's my big bro and he taught me a lot about the world today. He introduced me to the world, and to every new step in life. I followed right behind him. He broke the ice and I followed behind. Forget what everyone says. I know my brother. I know him like no one else does. I can understand what he said and what he meant. I wouldn't have followed through on such a strong feeling, though. But I can still understand how overwhelmed he felt – too much passion, not enough logic – all instinct, no brains. That's how he did it. That's what I learned from him. Just go. Don't think, just go. He got himself in the end, but damn did he live. No safety net, he just flew free. I always jump with a safety net. But I know why he doesn't. I know his heart. When you grow up with someone, you see the world through your own eyes and theirs. So I understand him. I wouldn't choose it, but I get it. Somehow, I get it. I know his heart and that's why I know he's still here. He taught me how to choose the free way, and my own structured way. He's the part of my heart that's free, because he taught me how to live that way. When I choose to jump without the safety net, that's Gabe. That's the part of my heart he developed. I like his free way. It wasn't my way, but I admired him because he had his way, even if it wasn't the 'right' way. I think he felt the same way toward me. My way wasn't his, but at least it was my own. Maybe this is why we could have mutual respect for each other. Each wanting to have our own way, yet have a piece of the others, the free spirit wanting a form of structure and the structured wanting a taste of the free. (Yin-Yang). My wild side, my fun, crazy, spontaneous side, that's him in me. That was his gift to me. Whenever I do something without the net, going against the current, following passion only, that's Gabe through me. I can feel it because that's what he taught me to be. That's the piece of him that I picked up by living life with him, and by his side. He called me "little miss perfect" with grades and following the rules and all that. Maybe he wanted to have some of that in him. I wanted to be freer like him. But neither of us could have transformed that opposite way; and we wouldn't have wanted to, not our style, not our heart. This opposite but mutual understanding must have been what kept us close, what allowed us to have a friendship,that, and God's grace. However, it's also what caused us to get into such terrible fights; straight differences. God, I am so grateful to have a big bro who taught me how to really live. Would have been better if he were here for a longer amount of time, but thanks to God that I got what I did from him, little punk. But I love him as a big bro and as a friend, and I respect him. Takes guts to do what you want and actually follow through with it. The heck with everyone. Do what you really want. So few do it. But he did. Messed him up in the end, but at least he did it. Each of us is the extreme on the spectrum. He being free and me being structured. I am so fortunate to have been blessed with a great big brother to have taught me how to keep my structure and how to really live; how to be free. He probably doesn't even realize he was doing that. Neither did I. But I realized it today. THANK YOU, GOD, FOR GABE

AND FOR LETTING ME BE THE BLESSED SISTER THAT GOT TO HAVE HIM AS MY BIG BROTHER. It has made all the difference in the world, and there will be few that will be able to touch my heart and my life the way he did. I love you Gaber Baber. Who better to teach me about life than the big brother that was there with me through it all?

~ *Thank you Lord for preparing my heart.* ~

❧ April 14, 2002 ❧

Last Wednesday (4/10) night I talked longer about it than I ever have before. I sat there with Mr. McFarlin and just went on and on for I don't know how long. Maybe an hour and a half or two hours. I don't even know, but it was a long time. And he just let me talk. We bonded that night. I finally let down my guard and was just being me. I cried in front of him, and I didn't care. I didn't feel embarrassed or ashamed. In fact, it actually felt good to cry in front of him just so he knows that I can be me, that he's so trustworthy of a person that I feel comfortable. I felt like we were really close friends then, and there wasn't another person in the whole world I would have rather talked to like that. It felt good to talk to someone that I know is older and wiser than I, and I thought could give me good advice. And he did. It just really touched my heart at how thoughtful he was. How he just listened to me. How he cared, and how he was there for me. Like how a true friend would be. He wasn't in a hurry to go anywhere, he was just listening. Ever since then it's like we've been closer. At least in my mind that's how it seems. Like I cut through all the garbage and just spoke too him like a friend; like someone on my same level; someone that understood me. I told him about so many things, things I never told anyone before because I just felt comfortable. I knew he wouldn't judge me. I would talk, then look at him for feedback or whatever, and I'll never forget the look in his eyes, just patience. Like I could go on forever and he would still be there. Gosh, it felt so good to get it all out. I had been holding a lot of it in since Easter, and that night I just let go. I had really wanted to talk to him about it, and it was like I was waiting for the right time. I don't know why him, why then, but it just was. Sometimes I only want to talk to certain people about certain things. And this week I wanted to talk to him. I'm just glad he was there for me and I can count on him. How it really started was I wanted to tell him thank you for coming to the funeral. I just wanted him to know that it was appreciated, and I remember seeing him there. And when I'm alone crying about Gabe's death, I remember the people that were involved in it; and that were involved in his life. McFarlin was one of those people, and I felt like I should let him know it doesn't go unnoticed that it meant a lot to me that my instructor and friend cared enough to be involved in my personal life. So when the studio was cleared out and I felt safe I started to talk. I told him that when you think something, you shouldn't hold it in. You should tell the person because you never know how long that person may be around. Then I told him that I really appreciated him being at the funeral. My lips were already beginning to quiver and I could feel the tears rising up just from me saying those words. Then he said you don't need to thank me for that, And when he said that I just wanted to cry so bad, but I didn't want to look weak. I wasn't ready to let my guard down yet. Then I explained how much it meant to me to see people from karate there. From that point on I felt free. I felt like I was talking to a good friend, and it felt so good that he wanted to listen. I was amazed at his patience. He taught me a lot by his silence. I felt so secure talking to him. Like he was a bro, and he was there for me. Somehow by spending thousands of hours over the past six years as his student, I feel like he knows me really well. In fact, part of that springs from the fact that I feel guilty about knowing someone for six years and not really knowing them for the person they are. So part of the reason was I wanted to let him into a part of my real life, not just my karate life. To know someone that long and not really know them doesn't satisfy me. I thrive off my relationships with other people. It's what makes me want to smile; knowing I can be there for other people and make them smile, too. So to know McFarlin for about six years and to only know him as an instructor and not a friend made me feel I didn't do my job. Like I didn't reach out to him; because I care a lot about him, and about everyone else I know, regardless of how well I known them. So by telling him about Gabe, that was my way of reaching out to him, to bring him into my personal life, to show him who I really am as a person, an individual, not merely a student. Plus, I just feel very comfortable with him, and I wanted to talk to him about Gabe. I wanted us to connect, and I wanted his advice because I respect him a lot. I figured he would have some good opinions. Dang, what a good friend he was to me that night. I need to learn to listen like that. I'm just glad there are people I can turn to for things like that. Now when we talk, I don't have to put on a front; I can just be me. He has seen me in my low time and so there's nothing to hide. So now even being at karate feels more comfortable because I'm more confident. Basically, that night was awesome for me because I again realized the significance of the saying, "Sometimes when you want to get a grip on things you have to learn to let go."

❧ April 18, 2002 ❧

I've been making a lot more entries lately. I guess a lot has been going on. Well, right now I'm thinking about a few things. I took Alex home from school today and somehow we started talking about everything with Gabe. She said a really nice thing that stuck in my head. She said, "He was such a dope guy, seriously. He had such a cool personality." Or it was something like that. She basically was commenting on what a cool person he was and how he was fun to be around. That's how I want to remember him. By saying that she reminded me of the person he was, both to me and to others. I'm so glad she said that so I could be reminded of that. We talked about Hume Lake and sneaking into the boy's cabins and all the other funny stuff. We talked about the good times. It felt good to talk about him, to remember him, in a positive way for a change. I told her sad stuff too, but my overall feeling was better than it would have been had I kept it all in. The second thing I have been thinking about has just been life in general. I feel like I'm growing up so much. Maybe that sounds dumb to say having only been alive for eighteen years. But nevertheless, the fact remains true. I feel like myself, as a whole, is changing and my beliefs and my personality are developing. I sometimes think life is so black and white, so clear. Other times I'm not so sure. Often I know exactly what I want, and I'm going to get it no matter what. Don't stop; get it, get it. Most of the time I do know exactly what I want; out of myself, out of life, out of just the day, whatever. And sometimes I feel so lost I don't know which end is up. So confusing! Often adults tell me I'm so focused, blah, blah, blah. Then why doesn't it feel that way? If I'm so focused then why don't I know the university I'm transferring to in two years? Why don't I know for sure what profession I want to go into? Why do so many people know, but I don't? I always have vision, direction, and goals. So why not now?

Why do I feel so young and yet so old? Why do I love being at school one minute, and the next I can't wait to graduate? Why do I feel so ready for the world, ready to attack it head on, but later I feel like I'd rather hide and not show the world myself yet? I think if I knew the profession I wanted to go into, half of these questions I would have the answers to. Anyway, maybe I'm just worrying too much. Either way, I know it will all work out in the end. It always does.

❧ *August 1, 2002* ❧

I've been feeling so sad lately. There's been so much going on with karate, and I've been faced with a lot of serious decisions. It saddens me so much to be going through all of this – I never thought I'd be leaving karate for something like this. I always thought it would be school that would pull me from the studio. I miss his presence in times like these because he would have a straight to the point, matter of fact way of handling it. He would have probably told me forget them, leave the studio – he didn't really like them anyway. I feel like he would have lightened up the situation. He would have brought humor into it and made me feel better. Why do I lose everything? He would have made this simple, would have made me not take it so serious. I miss his comments and the light-hearted way he handled things. I've been talking to so many people lately, and I don't hear his words in anyone else. He would have made me feel like the whole thing was much simpler than it was. When it all first started coming out and getting more serious, I felt the lack of humor he usually had in times like these. I felt his absence greatly. Just as I did today during mom's birthday when the whole family was together. Just as I did last Sunday on Darci and Luke's wedding day. I've thought about taking the sticker off the back of my car, several times... the sticker that reads: In Loving Memory of Gabe Williams. But I've never felt strong enough about it to follow through. Sometimes I feel his absence has made my problems greater. I feel like if he hadn't died, I wouldn't have had as much to deal with, and everything would be easier. Maybe that's false. Probably because I'd have a whole set of other problems to deal with. But that's how it feels sometimes. Like now. If he didn't die, I'd have a lot less to think, worry about. And all I'd have to worry about was the current problem; not the problem plus him being gone on top of it. It makes me so mad and sad sometimes.

How much less would I have to deal with if he were here? I'd have a lot less "on my plate." I don't have a big brother anymore. As much as I search for a replacement, none can be found – new brothers, new friends, but no replacements. None are even close to the personality and heart he had. I wish he was here to help me, to advise me, to help me cut through the garbage and see it clearly. He always did that for me, but now he can't and I face it alone. It feels so dead serious without him. Why, with something this important, is he not here? It's not fair. I didn't do anything to deserve this pain, yet I have to deal with it. He made the choice, but I live with the consequences – no punishment in heaven. It's not fair. I was forced to carry something I never volunteered for. It's not fair.

October 3, 2002

"Things I've Learned"

- think positive
- smile more
- the little things aren't so little
- pay attention to the little things; to someone else, they're big things
- treat everyone like they're a millionaire
- listen to the rain
- lay in the sunshine
- take the dog for a walk
- you will get hurt
- you will move on
- do it for you, not for anyone else
- love your friends
- love your family
- take a nap
- spend more time with people
- spend less time with things
- cherish the moment – it passes quickly
- pain only feels like it lasts forever
- make the extra phone call to brighten someone's day
- drink good coffee
- work hard
- laugh harder
- compliment others often
- take time to teach and to help

❧ *January 17, 2003* ❧

It feels like the damper has been put on the whole thing. It isn't what it used to be. It doesn't hold the same magic. All the luster vanished long ago. I feel like I've been fighting so long to attain something for which I no longer remember its once strong importance. I feel like I've been running against the wind, and now I'm tired. And I'm suddenly realizing, I'm the only one pushing myself to continue. And I wonder why it is I'm still pushing. I wish so much I could have what I used to have, the way I used to have it. It's hardly desirable anymore. I wish I didn't care about it so much; I could let it go so much easier. Maybe I should just continue. But what's the point? I don't even want to finish it. But maybe in the future when this time passes I will have regrets. I don't know anymore. Maybe I'll just start a new art or something. We'll see how it goes. I feel like I've already done so much, so why keep it going when I'm the only one pushing myself, and I don't even really want it?

❧ *Sunday, April 6, 2003* ❧

Today I became a third degree Black Belt. Shortly after leaving Tarzana Karate, Liza Hall called me and told me she talked to Mr. Altaie and explained the situation (my circumstances), and he wanted to test me. We emailed and spoke on the phone once. He agreed he would test me under certain conditions: one of them was that I understand I could pass or I could fail. He told me they do things an 'old fashioned' way, and as long as I agreed to that, that I could test. I agreed. I also learned right away that he was serious about what he did. So I knew I had to step it up. At his advice I worked out with Miss V (Von Monahoff) at Liza's house at least once, sometimes twice a week doing private lessons. I crammed and practiced every day from the time I knew I had a chance to test. And today that work has paid off. I can't believe it – I'm a third degree! This is something I have been looking ahead to for the past three years! And I was losing sight of it just a couple of months ago. But now, I'm here! I did it! I made it through a panel of seventeen Black Belts, a lot of nervousness, and some fear. But I did it! I feel so accomplished to have been able to test with such great martial artists – particularly on the panel: Mr. Altaie, Mr. Ercolono, Miss V, Mr. Silva, Mr. McDonald and many others. (And Josh was on the panel, too!) Mr. Altaie gave me some very nice compliments today. – He said it was a pleasure to teach me, and that I've fixed all the details he told me about. He also jokingly told me that the panel thinks I should kick a little higher! I laughed and told him I'd work on it, Sir! I feel so great to be a part of such a strong group of Black Belts. I feel so proud to have finally reached this point that I have had to work so hard to get to: leaving one school and moving onto others. But what a blessing it was to come to Tarzana Karate where I made the connections that have now led me to this day – third degree! My family, Chad and Cathey Long, and Travis and

Heidi Kemmer were there to watch me do it. And I made it! Just a tweaked ankle from a one step, but I did it. It felt so good to get that belt tied on me today. It feels like a huge chapter has been completed, and I'm so glad to finally reach this goal; and even better to feel like I really earned it. I've been on 'cloud nine' all day today that I just did what I've been wanting to do for so long. But at the same time, I feel sad that Mr. Altaie is leaving because we're all needing to find different places to train. There is one place in Chatsworth where one panel member told Mr. Altaie his Black Belts could use a new school he just bought and use it to work out in on Monday nights. I'm glad for that – and maybe we could continue to train at Liza's house every once in a while. Also, Mr. Ercolono offered/asked me to teach at his school – 'The Way' in Agoura Hills, which is where we tested today. He's a fifth degree, and seems to be a very smart, honest, and very good martial artist and person. Mr. Altaie said that is the highest compliment someone can give is that someone that high of a rank and that respectable person wants me to help teach his students. Later on he told me that he wished his students would have my kind of energy (I felt very good!) and he gave me his business card so I could contact him about teaching. I just felt so good about what I did today, and I feel so proud to be given my rank by such a good martial artist and a great panel. I just hope that everyone is going to work out together so we can continue to work and to train. (Especially Miss V, Ms. Hall (Liza), Mr. McDonald, etc that I trained with at Tarzana Karate). Anyway, I just had to write about this to contrast the last entry and so that I will never forget how I feel right now. Like I conquered something so great: rediscovering a new school, getting to be a part of such an awesome Black Belt family, and achieving this long range goal. I prayed for so much help/strength/God's presence in me on this test. And I got it. I did it, and I feel so great. I want to continue my training and my growth. The reason for the taped in scrunchie is because I picked an orange one this morning kind of thinking about Gabe. It wasn't a dominant thought, but it did enter my mind and served as a small source of motivation and remembrance. (I was busy thinking about other things – like focusing, praying, being confident, thinking positive, etc.) I did it! I'm a third degree and I have so many things to look forward to! Yeah!

❧ June 21, 2003 ❧

I wonder if I romanticized the relationship too much – in my memories, at least. Upon recalling events, conversations, etc., it seemed with each positive remembrance the bad ones were pushed further away. The more I thought about the great times we had, the more the regretful experiences were pushed to the back of my mind. I wonder if the things I was remembering came so great in number into my mind that they dominated my memory and effort to recall the unpleasant memories. Although I would like to think the good times we had, outnumber the bad, is it true? Sometimes when a person dies, even a villain, he/she is thought of as a hero. Did this spell cast over me also? Creating rose colored glasses with which I view my memories of him? I think I did. I wanted so badly to hang on to the things we shared, that's just about all I let my mind wander to. Perhaps in an effort to feel less guilty about grievances I may have caused him, and not wanting to feel the weight of the impossibility to express my regret to him about such experiences, I chose not to recall them. Because of this, these memories of my regretful behavior, fights, and cruel words toward him, have only recently revisited my mind. I was so masked and perhaps unwilling to face such regretful times, that I hardly remembered at all how many times he had caused me anger, bitterness, sadness, and tears. Because of this, these feelings resurfaced recently when I was overcome with emotion about his death and missing him. I was talking to Sara about it, and I could barely believe the angry emotions I had inside of me: anger directed at him at how rude and inconsiderate he used to treat me. I found myself recalling so many hard times where he made me feel angry and hurt. So many times he did this! To my joy, guiltily, I felt better about having lost him. It reminded me that my loss was not so great. It reminded me that I did not lose somebody who brought only joy to my life, as my previous memories had suggested. No, I lost somebody who brought both joy and pain to my life. Thus, by his loss, I was losing somebody who brought both ill feelings into my life and my family's lives. This was a feeling I have not yet experienced until now – his loss brought me a joy that reminded me that there are some good things about him being gone. Not just the things God has done to better a worse situation. But rather, with his loss, although much pain it has brought me, it has lessened the pain he used to bring. I don't fight with him. I will never have to yell at him, or block his punches: both literal and verbal. That is a relief. Although after this recent discovery, an unveiling rather, of the whole person he was, I felt I had a much better picture of him in my mind. It gave me more freedom. I was acknowledging both sides of the emotional spectrum that he brought into my life while he was living. I felt I mourned more thoroughly if that's possible. Although, my river of tears that have built up over the past three and a half years would seem to object. But that's what I conclude. By my cross examination of the positives and negatives, I decide that yes, I did suffer a great loss that is and was a struggle, but it was not a great, rose-filled happy memories relationship as I liked to remember it. Perhaps that is part of making the relationship last longer because he isn't here with me anymore. And since our relationship must be continued later (heaven), my way of prolonging it, renewing it, is to depict it in a much more positive light in an effort to make it last longer, extend it, enjoy it a second time. By doing so, I create a scapegoat for any regrets I may have, and I tell myself we had something better than we really did. It makes it easier to live with myself. Myself and my thoughts, my ideas about what I could have said or done, or not said or done. Whether a coping mechanism or not, my favoring the positive thoughts made me remember him only in a way I wanted to. Perhaps even assigning him characteristics he didn't possess in an effort to make him even better in my mind. Whatever it is, he was a great brother, and he also did drive me crazy at times. By expressing myself to Sara, it helped me to mourn all of him, miss him, the whole person that he was, a complex character definitely. By sweetly mourning the good times we shared, and by acknowledging the struggle of hurtful times, and reminding myself that I don't have to deal with those any longer, it brings me more comfort. And for the first time in a long time, I mourned his loss and was thankful for the end of the rough experiences we put each other through.

Although the whole mourning process is a rough experience, he has forced me through by his choosing to end his life. It is a completely different feeling. I felt so much more true to myself, and Gabe, when I was crying about losing him, reliving that, and missing him; much more true to myself when I recalled the painfully the memories we shared, even the painful ones, because it was real. And our relationship was real, a mix of these kinds of memories. Why would I mourn the loss of knowing we will have no more happy memories on this earth together? That is mourning only one part of him and his life. I learned that I must also mourn the unpleasant parts. It feels so much more complete to do so.

I have changed my views about talking about him, thanks to Josh and Sara. Josh tells me that I shouldn't be apprehensive about people asking who the sticker on the back of my car is for. He says I will get a good response from people if I act like it doesn't get me down. If I have confidence about it, then they won't feel awkward when I tell them it's my brother. Sara reminds me that I should be proud of my family, and that people will be responsive and sympathetic. She also tells me I'm not obligated to tell anyone I don't want to tell. She also reassured me that it doesn't look bad upon my family that my brother killed himself, although sometimes it feels like it reflects upon my family and me. I don't want that to be the first impression people get of my family. I think we're great, but we have problems like anyone else. But we have never had a problem quite as severe as this.

She tells me not to get hung up on this, that if they know me, they'll know that's not true. Also, that if they judge me based on that then ignore them. They don't get it. With that reassurance I am now prepared, even hopefully awaiting for someone to read the sticker and ask, "Who's Gabe Williams?" Because I will respond proudly with a smile that, "He's my brother." Sara thinks this will even maybe prompt questions from them as well as understanding, not a judging eye. I feel so much better now about who he was, and is to me. I now carry a picture of him in the gauges in my car tucked next to my gauges. I smile when I see it rather than shudder thinking about what questions it may prompt. I'm proud now, of who he is, my brother, a great fun person who brightened up everyone's days. Someone with great energy, who taught me to be the same and brought it out in me (energy which I express through the martial arts, and when I'm with people). He has taught me so many great things, and I'll never forget it. Now, I'll show it with a little more pride – my awesome big brother, Gabe Williams.

✥ June 26, 2003 ✥

It was the first time I had ever done it. I brought his name up. I used to never do that. I always heard the other members of my family bring up his name or an event he was involved in. In the past, such moments as those were met with uncomfort and hope that my eyes wouldn't meet theirs for fear they would await a response from me. But I felt so free when I was the one telling a "Gabe story." Why did I feel so awkward to do so before? Was I denying his importance in my life by refraining my memories of him when others shared theirs? Perhaps. All I know is I'm so glad I did talk about him – it made me feel so much safer, and to my surprise, I felt more security after sharing my story then I have these years previous when I didn't share my thoughts. I thought at the time that I was protecting myself, but when I let my guard down, I found the opposite. It was safer with my guard down as opposed to up. In my efforts to protect myself and my private thoughts, I think I did nothing but damage myself (by my lack of self disclosure). I can't believe I'm saying this – it's so counter intuitive to my previous beliefs.

My family was in the car and my dad said that he thought that was a good picture of him. (I had it tucked behind my gauges). I acknowledged him, saying it was one of my favorites. Then I told him and everyone in the car the story behind it. Then I reminded my mom the CD we were listening to was the same one we played constantly while in Missouri visiting him. I felt so open, and comforted by my own courage to let go. By letting go, I think I actually have a better grip. I'm stronger and I love it, and I love him and it's ok that he's not here. I'm alright with that. God is always with me which He shows me everyday. I am content, maybe for the first time, with this topic.

❧ *Wednesday July 23, 2003* ❧

It reminds me of you when I see a little boy with spunk, energy, It reminds me of you when I hear your laugh coming out of my mouth.

It reminds me of you when I do something out of character, when I go out on a limb and get a little more wild than usual; it's you coming out in me

I get excited for you when I see ugly things in the news, and anger between people. I think you're so lucky to be in so much of a greater place than I. You don't have to see what I see any longer. But I'm excited for me too, because I know one day I will join you also. Neither of us will have to see any more of what is cruel and cold. But you're lucky to have that now in a weird way.

It reminds me of you when I see a young brother/sister pair, ages like ours. I think of us. And I think of how we used to be that way too. So young and inexperienced, yet discovering our world side by side, knowing only ourselves and the world of our family. But I found a different world than you apparently. But your world was so much more exciting and fun, had more risk. But now with your death I have permission to take on "your" world, the world that was your reality. Now my world has more risk. More adventure. It is both my privilege and my obligation to carry on your characteristics, your world, in the reckless exciting way you saw it. I wanted to carry it on, yet at the same time I felt like it's now allowed. Before it wasn't. It was yours but now it can be mine. Since you're not here to live out that wild and fun side, then I can. I don't want your energy to die, I want it to stir up in me, inspire me, and it has. Now I gladly take it on. Because when I carry that energy, charisma, zeal for life, I carry you. Before you died, I wasn't allowed to be this way, not by my standards. After your death I realized I could no longer look to you and admire it. I must myself possess it; or it will die, and

I will not find it in you. And I don't want to find it in anyone else. It was your quality, but with your death I claimed it. It was a way for me to keep a part of you close – the part of you I loved the best. So I stored it in myself. Not in a freaky way, but in a love for you, preservation of your memory, way. I get happy when I feel that part of you coming out in me. I'm happy because I have something of yours. Rather, I'm happy because it is now mine, too. I have learned to use such a great thing you gave me. You taught me what to do, how to have that zeal. Now I have it, like you had it. You, your memory, drew it out of me, inspired me. If you didn't die it probably would have never come out. I would have admired the energetic quality from a distance. I would have never been inspired to bring it out in myself. Do you admire what I do from a distance? Probably not. You're in the best world ever! What do you need with this world? Although I wish you didn't die, and I would have you instead of myself gaining the use of a new quality. It would be far better to have you. But since I don't, I can be grateful that I'm finally using something you taught me to use. (But I never did use it until after November fifteenth, that's the important part). Your death brought it out in me.

I am especially happy because what was his philosophy of life, his energetic carefree approach, is now my version of the same thing. I have applied to my life what I learned from his and have made it my own. I have made it a part of me. He taught me how to live life recklessly. Take risk and smile while doing it.

✄ July 31, 2003 ✄

It's 2:31 a.m. – that might explain why this entry is so weird. What a strange place this world is. It is so complex, yet so simple at the same time. Imagine if the world were the same everyday – maybe God planned it this way so we would always have things to explore so we would never get bored. All in one day... I can have a great deep conversation, or contemplate the world, the future... yet also in that same day, I could have a conversation about caterpillars with a child. How can things change so much in such a short time? Change is good. Change leads to growth, growth leads to a better me. Emotions are such a weird thing, too. How can they be so rational, have such good timing and also be so off, so irrational? And why again do these opposites take place in such a short time? Sometimes I am in such control of them I surprise myself. Other times I feel as strong as a rubber band holding the weight of an elephant. Why is everything so weird and unpredictable? Well, at least it keeps things exciting. I am way too tired to keep blabbering like this. Sometimes I feel like a genius, other times like a six year old asking why the sky is blue. Strange.

P.S. I just remembered...

Mike Louthian told me the other day that he had a dream about Gabe. He saw him on the stairs somewhere and they were talking. Mike dreamt he had died then he saw him. I was touched by it because it means that Gabe is somehow in his subconscious thoughts, coming out in his dreams. Then I told Mike that I thought that was interesting that a part of Gabe is still in his mind. It's still a thought floating around, resurfacing. He said, "I know, even four years later." And that was the comment that really made me think. Mike was surprised to have a dream about Gabe because it was "four years later". He thought that because it happened so long ago, it was strange for him to still be thinking about it. Then it made me realize how very different the last four years have been for me compared to him. It is the interpretation of those years that separate me from him. He's my friend and I love him, but these last four (almost) years are the difference between night and day.

He's surprised to be thinking about Gabe after all that time, and I'd be surprised if I did not think about him every week or week and a half to two weeks. Talking to Mike made me realize again the wide gap between others and myself on this topic. For everyone else, it has been a mere typical passage of time. But in sharp contrast the last four years (thinking back to the time when he died) have felt like both an eternity and a short breath. All these times, I've struggled and I've felt these foreign complex emotions, and others have not. Those hidden unidentified, ever-changing emotions are what creates the Grand Canyon of separation between me and everyone else who doesn't feel it. Almost like they were enjoy

It was almost through Mike's interpretation of the last (almost) four years that made me realize just how different those years have been for me. To him it seems like such a long time ago, but for me I can remember that night like it was yesterday. Like the slow forming scab has cracked and blood seeps out. But I don't care because the "blood" is real, and facing it, nursing it, is so much better than ignoring it, covering it with a band-aid.

I couldn't believe it when I heard it. To him it had just been four years. He was just cruising. But to me they have been such a struggle, private victory, God really, which the outside world never sees. That's usually when it hurts the most. When someone says or does something and you think of him, but they don't know it. And even if you told the people around you, their understanding it first hand is so limited, so why even bring it up? But at times like that I hurt privately, alone, and that's when it hurts the most. Even though people are so great and they are really helpful, there is such a boundary that separates your pain from their ability to understand it. And you know they won't understand and they cannot help you lift your burden through their words. Although the effort is appreciated, the depth of understanding is so shallow compared to the deep, deep depths of hurt and of pain. The kind word of others, though meant well, is like a band-aid being offered to a patient in the ER whose wounds require five pounds of gauze. That is when it hurts the most. When there is a remembrance of him, I remember it alone usually because what's the point of sharing? Only I will truly appreciate it. It hurts the worst to hurt alone knowing people are kind but that they really don't understand. Because my love is deep, the loss of that person I love makes my sadness and longing and pain equally deep. I am reaping what I sowed; I sowed love and a good relationship. But now that it's gone, I will also feel that great pain and loss. But I do not regret sowing that love. Although the difficult times are when you feel an emotion that is exclusively yours, or an inside joke comes to mind that only you would understand. I do find comfort. But it is not of the flesh. It is from the One who conquered death. I am coming closer and closer to Him and He amazes me everyday. Especially by his love, faithfulness, and numerous answered prayers. I always find hope. But that doesn't mean I didn't find hope through much suffering; working through the pain. I told God today that if Gabe had to die in order for me to know Him like I do now, it would be worth it. It wasn't a trade, but it's what came out of it. I leaned on God, and I've been getting to know Him better and better and have a genuine relationship with Him. Before Gabe died I didn't have that. I lost someone I love so much, but in return I gained a relationship with the One who is Love and who created love. Pretty good what God can do with a difficult situation. He amazes me everyday. Today I actually thanked Him for what happened because it brought me closer to Him.

So I do find comfort, even when all the pain sears through my heart. I always, always find comfort.

❦ *September 14, 2003* ❦

It places you in a class of your own. It makes you auto-matically retain a pair of glasses through which you can only see the significant and all else fades away. Only what's important, what's really important in your life, stays. Everything else falls by the wayside and you think, "Who cares?" It separates you from other people, and the seemingly insignificant daily tasks which plague their small-minded conversations. It's as if you were given amazing wisdom and insight into life, and everyone else is in a dream world. You have a bird's eye view and they're completely blind. It makes you realize what's important in life, and all you want to do is be with people you care about and nothing else holds any weight. EVERYTHING else can wait. What once seemed important is now tainted because now you have a serious hurting heart that aches with something so real, so true. It makes you see how fake the world really is, and how its not centered on what really matters. And you realize you are very withdrawn from this fake, safe place which you once were a member of. It hurts to know you're trying to deal with the loss of a loved one, so real, such true genuine feelings, and the rest of the world doesn't get it. They're still concerned with their own agendas. Driving fast. But I know I must tend to my wounds. They're too deep and real to be nursed by fake doctors from a fake, impersonal world. I can hardly stand to look at anything around me when I miss him. My feelings are far too genuine to be entertained by such a super-ficial world that knows nothing of reality – of real pain. It really places you in an elite class. You know what life is about, and they don't. It's about the people you love, and when they leave, you really realize that. From that point on, you appreciate what is real: your love for them, your pain in response to losing the reciprocal expression/giving/receiving of that love. When something hits you that deep in the heart, it is difficult to appreciate all other forms of what you thought you used to love; they only skim the surface, and it is a cheap imitation. Nothing else will satisfy such a deep hunger. That's what makes it so difficult sometimes. When my heart hurts and I miss him, I realize that my heart is going through something so deep, so hurtful, that nothing else going on around me is important. Food and air are second to it. It's that deep. People who haven't felt that kind of depth don't really understand how important it is to nurse the wounds when they reopen. That's what sets me apart from people. I'm talking life and death, they're talking, "Chinese or Mexican for lunch?" No comparison. The good thing though is that it grounds you. When I get caught up in my life and I see something and I get a remembrance of him, I am again grounded and reminded of what is really important. Then I'm glad I'm spending time with friends and other important people to me. His death has added so much meaning and understanding. Rather, it has revealed to me how important the people, not things, are in my life. I feel such deep pain, but that reflects how much deep love I had for him that four years later I still miss him this much. Hit me like a wave today, I was missing him so much. Confused at what had happened and why it did. Reflecting on how fast it all happened. After the many, many tears, I felt comforted. Because I prayed but also because if I hurt this much, it's because I loved him that much. His former presence was so significant that even after all this time his absence is still noted. That did give me some comfort. I still wish so much that he was here. I expected him to be here today and everyday, and I took it for granted. I miss him so much. I miss not having him around for all the little things like just being home. Seeing him at home. Having fun with me, teasing me, talking to him. Getting comfort when I was mad at mom and dad, and when he was too. I wish he were a part of our lives. It was surreal. I looked at his gravestone, and I still had to ask myself, was that really him? Did this really happen to me, to my family? I wish I could hear his voice. Wish I could laugh at whatever he would say that would, of course, cheer me up, make me feel better. He was good at that. I was glad to feel the pain today, to be reminded of how much he was to me. Because if he wasn't, I wouldn't be feeling that. I miss the relationship and the friendship we had. It was so unique, it cannot be recreated. That idea is both comforting to know he can never be replaced, and it's also depressing when I want so much to rekindle that relationship in another. At least I know I will see him again one day, and until then the remembrances of him will bless me.

❧ August 16, 2003 ❧

The other day when I wrote that I cried harder than I can ever remember crying. It was like I was asking all the why questions again, only so much later. It was the first time I really asked, "Why?" and questioned God. I asked the first question last. And perhaps with more meaning this time. I really let go. I stopped caring about what control I had over my feelings and my desire/need to move on, carry on. I let go and I was sixteen again, back in the same spot emotionally where I started the grieving process. I asked 'why' again, but this time with more meaning. As much as I think I understand it medically, logically, I don't. I don't understand it because it's him. I know/knew him so much better, I don't understand it, though. I know the explanations the "professionals" give on the topic. They're the experts, they know that area well. Following suit then, I'm the expert on Gabe. I know him well. And the two don't match. To me, he was so different and unique as a person. How could he fit the expert's examination categories that explain why/how he could take his own life? To even write the words is strange. Unique he was; orthodox and standard fitting he wasn't. So how can the books and experts explain his behavior so well? He couldn't fit into many boxes, so how can he be boxed into a theory or explanation upon his death? He lived outside the box for everything, so does he really fit into what is a "normal case"? Was his planning/choice of death really so similar to others who committed suicide? He didn't fit the box on anything else, why this? Of course, it's like winning the lottery – you never think it will happen to you, your bother, your family. Maybe it isn't all that irregular after all. Gabe, why did you go out like that, then? They say your symptoms were the same as any other – same with your method. Your prior behavior, giving away of personal belongings, loss of hope, etc. If you were so unique like I thought you were, then why did you give up like everyone else, in the way they do? You live thinking outside the box all the way up until the end, and then you let them group you, categorize you. Say it was like others who have done the same. Did you tire of resisting conformity? So ironically when you let go, die, are you then conformed? So original until your death, then the books and the experts show that your death was so similar to the ones before you. That's messed up. Is that really it, though? I loved how you were so original during your life and hated how you were so packaged afterward. I wished so much that I could stand up for you and show people the truth about you when they would tell a construed account. But I couldn't speak up and change their minds. I was too desperate to cling on to my own impressions and remembrances of you. I wasn't about to waste my breath on someone who thought they knew you but only saw a piece. Throughout your seventeen years, I was witness to sixteen of them, and I thought that was warrant enough to mentally give me the victory over the others about testing/sharing their knowledge of you. I didn't need to fight. I chose not to. Let them have whatever memories, and I'll have mine, even if the two do conflict. I missed you too much to care if some people had some bad images of you. All of my energy was conserved to tackle the heartbreak and shock. And to pray for strength to do the above. Although most of that battle I didn't need to fight in, not for strength nor for comfort. My Father took care of that. He carried me much of the way, especially when I got tired, He got stronger. If Gabe hadn't have died I wouldn't have had the personal relationship I have with the Lord now. It still hurts though. It hurts because I miss his smile and his humor. I miss the private relationship we had – the one that no one saw when we would talk and when he would compliment me. And I know if I heard a compliment from my brother, he meant it! Unless he wanted money from me. I miss that most because no one saw it, and therefore there are no separate accounts to recall it or relive it with. In private the relationship was built, and so it cannot be duplicated because there are no other eyes that saw it. So in private I miss that relationship. No one saw it, no one knew our closeness, so alone I must mourn it. I see him in karate students sometimes. They have his punches, his movement. And so I remember that part of our relationship too. We had so much mutual respect for one another in that way and he told me so. We would spar each other so hard though! I miss him. He was an awesome friend and brother. I miss both of him.

- loud
- happy, smiling
- liked small things, miniature sample sized anything
- Nike shoes
- pants that were too big
- leaving his spoon in the ice cream container
- having his hair perfect
- energy
- friendliness
- loud laugh
- drug his feet when he walked
- blue N.C. Tarheels hat
- liked Jamba Juice ("Raspberry Rage")
- protected me – overprotected me
- protected my friends – said they were like his little sisters; said he knew them when they were two feet tall
- pushing the limits
- drinking straight out of the carton
- loved football – playing and watching
- Dolphins – Dan Marino
- he was fun
- he didn't like school work
- he wanted to get to elementary school before it started so he could play
- sometimes a jerk
- acted like he didn't know me in the hallways at school – unless he needed a dollar

Now I just wish I could hear his voice again – even if he was just asking for money. His voice and his smell were so hard to lose because they cannot be duplicated or be heard/smelt again in a passerby. I still have a shirt of his that hasn't been washed. When he first died I was so scared to lose it, to lose all the things around his room and his clothes that smelled like him. I was scared to see his clothes (some of them) to be given away; I knew his smell would become the first thing/remembrance of him that would go. I knew it would pass quickly, and I was so scared to think how rapidly it would pass. A few loads of laundry: clothes, sheets, etc., and his smell would be gone. I was so full of pain, watching how things would change, how his room would change, and I could do nothing. I would lose parts of him, one by one starting with his smell. I wished so badly that everything would stay the same, his room, his clothes, his closet and dresser. Almost thinking that if it all remained in tact he would feel closer. – Hey, he might even come back to it. That's the beginner's mentality. But I do remember feeling so sad that his smell and the look of the room would soon be gone – all too soon. It was fleeing so quickly from me, and I could do nothing to stop it. The best solution would be to bring him back, but I couldn't, though my heart desired it. Instead I settled for the shirt. – I could preserve a part of it for myself even though I couldn't preserve his room, the part of him left behind. I'm so mad my mom and dad let people take some of his clothes and use his room for storage. It's all we had left of him and they gave it away. His room will never be the same again, it will never look as he left it. Too bad. The car magazines and shoe space by the window has been replaced with gift baskets and Christmas decorations. Cheap replacement. Things we can put anywhere have replaced all the things he had left. It's a lack of thought to not preserve a memory of him that need not have been given away. I watched as people slowly took away his things and diminished all he had left. Well, at least I got a sweatshirt I wanted. Someone was going to try and take that, too. Well, it's not their fault. My parents let them do it; shortsightedness on their part. They were helping to comfort others and let them have something that reminded them of him. Instead of thinking ahead about who really is going to be hurting in the long run; and who could have used such objects as motivation and perseverance. Or at least for the sense of still having a piece of him – not all is lost. You can hold something close and be reminded of him, comforted. Remember that he's not too far away, and we will see him again some day. Whatever, what's done is done. I just wish I could walk into his room and be able to see that it once was his room. To be reminded that we haven't forgot him, haven't just turned his room into storage, and taken advantage of newly available space. How compassionate. How respectful. It would have been nice if we kept in tact the part of him we still had. But oh well. We have other aspects of him that are non-materialistic. But it's nice to have an abundance of both. Although in the long run it's him as a person that I really remember and hold onto. And of greater importance that his smell and his clothes are how I choose to remember him and be grateful for the things he did give me. Because it is both his life and his death that I respond to that really shape how he has affected me so powerfully.

❧ September 8, 2003 ❧

It resides around you, ever present, and will resurface at times, feeling so powerful. Other times it drifts away, seeming to be so distant, that you wonder if you'll ever feel the pain again. And you even wonder how strong it really was that it can be swept from memory so effortlessly. It is always there, though; the memory, the thoughts, the pain. Sometimes in the foreground, sometimes in the background, gray and void. I may remember it after I hear a person say the word, "suicide". I even dislike writing it, I used to hate even more reading it, coming across it by accident. The author never knowing the blade they had so swiftly pierced me with, and never meaning to do so. And into the hole, I tumble. It brings such a weight, just that simple word. Even worse was to hear it. That would be like being penetrated with a double-edged sword, even more powerful. To hear it brought horror, and I certainly wouldn't say the word. So hearing it inflicted a similar damage as if I were the one that uttered it. The word made me so uncomfortable, that their comfortable use of it made me even more uneasy. It held no power over them that use it. It doesn't make them recall memories they tried to handle in a timely manner, nor did it bring out to mind reserved emotions. The kind that alter one's concentration, as it did mine. But I have chosen to hear it differently now. Not to recall my own experience when I hear it, but instead to see it as a broader concept, unrelated to me. Instead, related to society in general, a social problem, not my personal one. It helps, but it is very difficult to block out my own heartfelt emotions that are attached to that word. To deny its affect on me lets me, momentarily, to be in the outside world, the world that has no emotional connection to it. Gives me a kind of liberation from it., a psychological tool that allows me to handle it, to not let it creep up on me and demand my attention, my painful recollections. Rather this change of mindset allows me when to decide when I will think about it, when I will deal with it. But it (pain, remembrance) always finds me outside of the book, classroom, or conversation after its conclusion. It's always waiting for me right outside the door.

September 9, 2003

At times I have to try hard not to look for him in other people. I have to focus on not trying to recreate what we had with another person I meet. Often, more often than I like, I meet someone who fits so well into the big brother role. And I desire a relationship like the one I had with him. I need it, and I feel neglected without it. This is when I realize I'm meeting someone, and I'm looking at them like they're a big brother. While I'm not looking to replace him, I am looking for some fulfillment to fill the void he left. I'm not looking for him, just any person that I feel that bond with. Someone to share that position with, kind of. It's not him I'm looking for; rather I'm looking for some form of that prior relationship to take place. The big bro/little sis relationship. And then I feel ashamed. Ashamed when my conscious mind catches up to what my subconscious mind is doing, what it's trying to recreate. I'm just looking for some kind of fulfillment in that way. And I feel that longing in my heart every time I meet someone and I feel us bonding in that way. I want us to have that kind of relationship. But I always realize that what I feel deep down, isn't just looking for a cool person to fill that big brother-type shoes. It's more than that. It's me missing him, missing our relationship that we had. And I won't be able to duplicate that in another person, nor do I want to. But I do find myself, nonetheless, searching for a substitute relationship to at least subside, if not appease, my hunger for that bond lost. There is a definite void. I recognize the times when I feel myself bonding with someone, in that big brother way, and I have to make an effort to see such a person in their own light. Not as a potential actor in my play. But I have to make sure I'm developing a relationship with them based on how we interact, and based on the qualities of Gabe I see in them. I have to work on appreciating them for who they are, and the friendship we can make. Not what I see in them and the big brother I wish they could be to me. It takes an effort to see them on their own terms, as they are, and not the way I wish we could be. I feel the void and I must resist the need to place people in it. I must resist the desire to assign meaning and feelings to people for which there is no merit for the assignment.

Katie and Gabe, ages 8 and 9

❧ September 12, 2003 ❧

Yesterday was the two-year anniversary of 9-11. I watched T.V., saw pictures and videos online, and I heard an incredible account from a man who survived, who worked in the towers, played on Focus on the Family. It was amazing to watch it, and remember those feelings. It especially hits me because I feel so much pain for the families. The people who like me lost their brother. I realize it's only been two short years, two long years, since they've passed. I remember all too well what the two-year mark feels like. I remember how short two years can feel, and I also know how long it can feel: how much you miss the person still, and how extremely powerful the anniversary of their death can be. I hurt for them, the families, and I pray for them because I somewhat feel a connection to those people all the way in New York. There was a shooting at Taft High School also. I was trying to get to the 101 freeway to get to karate, and I saw the flares the cops were putting on the street. As soon as I saw the flares I was taken back, to years previously when I saw the cops using those same flares to block off the street where my brother died. I remember getting dropped off at my aunt and uncles house. We were rounding the corner to turn on to their street, and I saw them placing them on the ground. At the time I thought they were still looking for him, and I thought for a split second, "Are those flares out for Gabe?" Then I realized, no, they can't be. It wouldn't make sense for them to go to that length for a runaway. But later I looked back on that and I realized that by that time he was already gone. When I drove by Taft and saw those flares it brought me back to that time. And I also remembered how heavy it makes the air at a school when something like that happens. So I felt that pain for them. It seems like so many places I go I see remembrances of him, or more often of "it". "It" is his death and my grief. Thinking about him and thinking about "it" are very different. Thinking about him usually leads to thinking about "it", however. I remember him and the cool things about him, but I also haven't seen him in a very long time. Lately so many things remind me of him and "it", or just the latter. It kind of makes me feel alone, in the sense that I'm separated from other people when I think of it. It's a private battle going on in my head, and what will take precedence. I don't know. It will be either the past, his memory, or the present, my daily tasks and activities with other people. I used to wonder why I didn't think about it that much, like I went through a dry spell. Both my mind and my eyes were dry. He was far in the background, a subconscious thought at most. But now it seems to be the opposite. I cannot figure out why he has come up so often in my thoughts. I've been seeing so many things lately that remind me of him. It confuses me, yet fascinates me at the same time. I have been going through more changes lately, with choosing a future school for me, Josh going away to school, new karate school, school starting up again, etc. With stress these emotions follow close behind. They come out in times of stress and change, so maybe that's all part of this recent surge of thinking about him, and feeling the emotions surrounding that. I don't know. Part of it might also be my need to address the emotions, and my desire to understand, and thus minimize them. Desire to minimize the pain, to understand myself, to fight the battles now so that they will be reduced to small conflicts, rather than large scale battles. I need to minimize them because it takes its toll on mind and body.

❧ *September 28, 2003* ❧

There we sat in the comfort of the kitchen, she sipping her iced tea, me eating cheesecake. It was good. We got to talking and she asked me something, I don't remember what, and it spurred a conversation about age. And she asked me how old he would have been and I said twenty-one. Then she asked me, "So how are you doing with that by the way?" And I looked down at my plate, thoughtfully at the raspberries I had picked from my food, wanting to give her a truthful answer. She mistook my glace perhaps because she followed her first question with, "I'm sorry, it's probably a stupid question. Of course it's hard." And I said, "No, it isn't a stupid question." The truth is I wish people would ask more often. Sometimes it seems people have forgotten about it. Truthfully, I answered her. I told her that sometimes it's really hard and I can't get it off my mind and I'm wondering why I'm feeling it so particularly strong at that time. Other times I'm not thinking about it at all and it's sometimes hard to imagine that only so recently I felt the opposite. I told her that it affects me differently every day. I told her that each time I think of it, or it affects me, I feel a different emotion. Sometimes I'll look at something in a store, or drive by a particular place, and I'll think happily, "Oh, that's like something he would have liked, or that is something he did like." And that thought and the ones that follow it lead me to think a certain way and to feel certain emotions. And another day I will see that same thing or something like it and I'll think, "I wish he was here to see it." That's the saddest part about it for me. And each time something comes up I feel something different. It's a different emotion, yet through my interactions with people, and because each day is different from the next, it holds different things in it. Thus different emotions are held in it. I will feel a certain way on some days rather than others because that day in itself is different. The time of day, the weather, the people I saw, the things I have to do that day, etc. It all affects how I will feel that day with regard to this. I told her that the pain I feel will manifest itself in different ways via different emotions. Throughout the nearly four years that have passed I wonder if I have ever felt the same emotion twice. I don't think I have. Every day, every experience is so different, and it will continue this way for the rest of my life. One day when I'm older and married and have kids, I will wish he was there to be their uncle. This list of examples goes on. The past pages prove this; every time I encounter a new situation, I miss him in a different way, thus feeling a new emotion with each experience. It's like a whole other life within my big life. It is definitely a new life and sparks new growth spiritually. But I'm, OK with that. I know that I have grown closer to God because of this, and He has led me so much closer in His direction as a result. He has made me a better person and I've discovered His love, and peace that surpasses all understanding. Yes, I have to deal with a lot of pain and loss to a depth that many people will never understand. But that's alright. Those people who don't know pain like this can still grow closer to God in other ways. And those people who don't know the depth of this pain will have in its place many peaceful days – days not filled with the pain I have known. Again, I am OK with this. Jesus sees me through the pain – and I learn so much about Him, me, us, and His love in the process. I consider it a fair trade because now I have known more growth and greater love and fulfillment than ever before. I have had to become a master interpreter of my emotions. I told her the reason I think people hurt so much is they don't understand their emotions. Having such a variety and always ever changing emotions/feelings has made me develop the need to decipher them. If I understand them then I can address them and fix them. I can deal with them if I can recognize them. I think many people hurt needlessly, more than is appropriate, because they don't look within themselves and try to understand what and why is going on inside them. Ultimately I think God is the Healer, and He can address our pain. But how can we even take that first step toward our healing, and our Healer, if we don't even understand what's going on inside us? This is what I told her and she liked it. Basically, if I understand my pain, and my emotion, then I can deal with it. How can I heal if I don't even know the source of my pain/my wound? How will I know what needs help? How will I know what to ask Him for? I like to be specific in my prayers so I know when they're answered – so my analytical side can't take over and doubt the result. So I feel that if I can come to my Lord in prayer about my needs, and about my pain, I'm one step closer to the remedy. He ultimately is the One who will heal me, but if I mentally can detect the source of the problem/the pain, I can get to work on it. I just have to honest with myself about that pain. When I'm honest with myself and God in prayer, I get the best results, the best healing. This tells a lot about my relationship with Him. I bring to Him my struggles, do the best I can with it, then bring it to Him and let go. He always does a better job than me – but I'm just grateful that He is so willing to help. Like He's been just waiting for me to bring it to Him, because He always takes care of me. Sometimes immediately, and sometimes He holds off and does what's best for me in the long run. Either way, He always has the solution. No matter what way I'm feeling sad, or what way I'm missing Gabe, He's right here. Ready to take me in, ready to accept me, help me, strengthen me. strengthen me to strengthen others. I feel a deep need and desire to help others. I feel that even though I've had this big event of my brother's suicide shake me up and change my life, I've still had it easy. I've had one big thing to deal with but the rest of my life has been filled with so many beautiful blessings, who am I to complain? Who am I to hold back and not help others? I don't feel I've had it like others have had it. Some people have lived their whole lives dealing with this heavy kind of pain. And I have had only one main experience of this kind of pain – and even then I have had tremendous help from my Heavenly Father to deal with it. So even in my pain, I won't complain. I have had it pretty good despite the loss of my brother. I doubt anything else in my life will ever affect me as much as this has – both positively and negatively. Laurie told me that she has felt similar pain about her daughter who has special needs. She feels the pain and the loss and the struggle that goes along with that challenge. She also feels that sense that her pain is so deep, the rest of the world just doesn't "get it". They don't know the depth, and the pain, and how it resurfaces with each new experience, with each new year. Although she claims to never understand the deep pain I go through with Gabe, I think the same thing about the pain she experiences. And yet it is so similar in the sense that the pain is so real, so deep – depths it reaches that other people don't understand. How appropriate, isn't it, that also the depths of God's love we cannot fathom, just as others cannot fathom the depth of our pain. She also finds comfort in His strength. It seems she walks close to Him and relies on Him – it's inspiring. I wish I could tell everyone how awesome God is and how much He has done for me and therefore how much He can do for them. In a way, I'm so glad I had to go through all this pain – so I can know Him and walk with Him in ways that I never did before Gabe died. As Laurie put it, "Now you rely on Him." Exactly. And it didn't even hurt to write his name – it used to hurt just to say or write his name, Gabe. But it doesn't anymore. That's the kind of growth and healing, and definite strength He has given me. Laurie talked about this for so long with me tonight. – I told her all about how the different emotions affect me, and what I experience. She was amazed at how complex it was, and how it is ever changing. I never thought about it from that perspective – it seemed obvious to me, that's what would happen. Of course my emotions would change with the days and times and events in my life. But looking at it from her view, I'm learning once again.

She said she went to the doctor and they looked at her heart for a long time. She has an extra valve in her heart. This explains why every six to nine months her heart will beat rapidly out of control for about forty minutes. And the doctor said he has never seen anything like this before, and he is very interested to figure out what it is. They, the doctors, are going to take a look at it and figure out if this extra valve is a good thing or a bad thing. And when her heart does the rapid beating only she can really feel it because it is within her. But other people can see it pounding in her chest, even see it pulsating. This struck me. The heart condition parallels very similar to my experience regarding Gabe. It is internal, and only I can feel it, just like her heart beats. And she doesn't know exactly when it will start, only that it will come, and it will affect her. Just like I know I will get another remembrance of him, and it will likely affect my whole day. (If it's a powerful one!) People can see her heart jumping in her chest and people can see my sadness and my downcast spirit (sometimes). Other times it's undetectable except to a few people. And also, it is speculated by the cardiologists whether or not this valve is a good thing. Well, it could also be looked at as questionable if Gabe dying was a good thing or not. It's all in your perspective. I say Gabe dying was not a good thing for me. It's an "extra" thing I carry in my heart, just as she carries an "extra" valve. I would say that his death was bad, but the after-effects were good. I have grown so much as a result of his death, so optimistically I say it was a good thing despite the pain I have endured. As for Laurie's valve, she doesn't know yet if it's a good thing or a bad thing. I suggested to her that it was a good thing – that maybe it means she'll live to be 137! =) I don't know. But either way, it's all a choice of perspective. I didn't choose to have my brother die and be out of my life. But I choose to think optimistically anyway, and to keep looking ahead keeping my eyes on Jesus. I was fed spiritually tonight through her our conversation and through her words. She told me that she felt she needed to tell me to publish this, and that I could inspire people. I told her it's just a bunch of entries about my emotions and about death. She said death inspires people. You don't have to tell me! It just inspired the last five pages! (With God's help, always). If my words can help people, then I want to use them for just that purpose among other things. God doesn't make mistakes. He could have stopped Gabe from dying, but He didn't. That wasn't a mistake. And if out of this can come an ability for me to help people, to understand their pain and show them God who can help them through it, then it will have served a purpose. It's not my doing, it's God's. I think this is the only entry I've ever made without crying. Again, there's God, strengthening me. I'm feeling His purpose – just as I prayed and asked for today. And He gave it to me – He answered my prayer. He never ceases to amaze me. He's awesome and I'm so glad I know Him. I really connected with Laurie tonight and we both felt like we were on a spiritual high, we were so connected. We were both feeding off each other's words, and I felt the Spirit moving in between us – in a way so powerful and moving, a way I don't recall ever experiencing before in this kind of way. God answered my prayer powerfully tonight by giving me this, spiritually feeding me when I was hungry.

This process has been a Journey of the Heart.

❧ October 2, 2003 ❧

I sat on the bench, red-faced and pouring with sweat. I took off one glove then the other. I unvelcroed my foot and shin pads, took off my headgear. I took my mouthpiece out and put it back in the case, returned all my gear into my bag. As I did so I looked at the big whiteboard hanging on the wall to my right: "Red and Black Belt Testing – Sat. Nov. 15". Sarcastically I thought, "Oh great." And with such a simple line, the date really, I plunge into thoughts questioning what I will do. It's the anniversary of his death. Will I go to the test? I don't finish the thoughts right then and there, but I know they will resurface as soon as I have time to think alone. I had to go back out on the mat. I glanced away and focused on the rest of class. It has passed out of my mind and by the time I got home I was just thinking about the studying I had to do. Then I sat there reading the karate newsletter for October and it also had the calendar on the back for November, and I saw it in writing again. And the same feelings cam back again – I thought, what am I going to do? And I wonder will I go to the test – it's a big one and I really want to go – but where will my head be? Will it be hard for me to focus, will I be wishing I wasn't there, wasn't putting myself through something? Ahhhh! This is what I don't like about this! I'm wondering what I will feel like on that day, the day he died, four years ago. This is horrible. I don't even know how to approach it... I really want to go, but I don't know how I might feel that day. Thinking rationally, it's only October 2nd! Why am I already anticipating this? I think, of course I'm going to the test! Why would I sit here and try to decide whether or not I'm going to go – it's over a month from now! Who cares?! Why am I even thinking about this? Why is this even an issue? Then I think all this is stupid – I'll just take it one step at a time. If this day draws near and I think I'm going to want to be alone that day, then I won't go. Or if I'd like to be a little distracted that day, then I'll go. I probably will go. I dunno, this really is not that big of a deal. I'm not going to let that one day of the year dictate my actions on that day for the rest of my life. But the thing is, the time, the countdown until then is in my mind. I feel the seasons changing, and I know it's close. It's like negative anticipation for that day. Like any other day I get excited about coming, my b-day, whatever. You feel the weeks until it arrives. This is the same way, but you're not excited it's coming. But you can't deny it, you know it'll hit you, so you can't hide. But you don't want it to come, but you do so that it will pass. And with time comes healing. I have to go to class, I'm gonna be late.

❧ October 20, 2003 ❧

I watched it last night and it moved me like I never would have thought. It felt emotionally, that I was knocked over. I watched the videotape of his funeral. I think my dad had someone tape it, I'm not sure. The tape showed everything – all the people, so many, I think around 700 or so. It followed his casket down the center isle, showed the people who spoke and sang, our pastor from when we were little, my aunt, and one of his former Sunday school teachers sang. One of the pastors that knew him also spoke – it was so touching, Pastor Pete Van. All the people that shared time on the microphone to tell stories, all of these created a cumulative affect on me. I remembered the day so well – too well. It was real. It's hard to explain. It was like time travel. I was back in that chair at church, feeling everything again – only more powerful this time. Yet some things were less powerful. It's like reading a book numerous times – each time you read it you come out with something different; more emphasis on some points less on others. Watching this video felt like emphasis was greater on every point. It made me miss him so much more – I felt it again just as I did on that day four years ago only this time with a bird's eye view. Hearing the people on stage sharing their stories was what hit me most powerfully I think. I remember so clearly that time – the time when the house was so full of people, full of helpful people bringing food and comfort. Back when everyone was in pain. But now it's only me, and I'm not "allowed" to be as mournful now as I was then. No person has ever told me this, but still I know how it is. In some ways I have these expectations for myself just like I perceive the world has them of me. I'm supposed to be calm and collected by now. Miss him, but not let it affect me too strongly. Again, no one has ever communicated this to me – but still, I feel I have to move on – take big steps. Actually, upon closer examination, I put this pressure on myself. It's not influence from others. Others are compassionate when I bring him up. It's my own pressure on myself to grow and to survive this, to survive this pain. So in my mind I urge myself to press on, to try hard to move on. But watching that funeral tape for the first time brought me back to a time when mourning was OK. It was more than OK – it was EXPECT-ED. It was totally OK to feel the pain. Socially it was accept-able and to me it was acceptable. But my world, society, whatever, pushes me to get over it, to move on. And I have. But that videotape brought me back to a time where everyone supported me. Where are they now? At the time when the house was always so full of people, it was almost too much attention. It was overwhelming. But where are they now? Now is when I really need all those people – this is exactly the time when I need them. Everyone told me to call them if I needed help – they told me anytime. Does that still count? Of course I still talk to my close friends about it – but what about all the people who were so close-by in the beginning? I wish there were more people around now – for more comfort. Although I must say a lot of the time when I miss him I want to deal with it alone. Me and Christ of course, but I like it that way sometimes and I feel it gives me more strength. Strength for the times when people aren't available, or when something else must take precedence over my mourning. I hate those days. Days when the schedule takes over when all I really want to do is sit and cry about it. Days when I'm so down but must go do something – go to school, study, teach karate, whatever. Those are times when I fully rely on Christ. I don't have the strength, but He does. I don't have the ener-gy or the resources, but He does. So I ask Him, and He gra-ciously and bountifully gives me the strength and the resources that I need such as today. I had to go to my photog-raphy class, then leave early and go to the transfer center, to learn about applying to universities, then go to my journalism class. After that I had to go home and change, go teach a karate class, then drive to my Grandpa's b-day dinner, then go to church at 7:00pm. Whew! So much! I didn't have time to rest today, so I had to rely on God too give me rest. Once again, He was faithful. That's just how amazing He is to me – always taking care of me. He always cares for me. I'm not complaining about my schedule – I say all the details to show the complexity of the day. The kind of complexity that a fragile spirit can't handle, on top of the deep sadness of missing a loved one. And with such a fragile, mourning heart and spirit, an upset in the day causes so much stress and heaviness of heart. But although I was filled with sadness, the Lord filled me with joy. Joy and faith in Him to get me through the day. A complex day, the kind that would upset my fragile spirit if I wasn't walking with Him. But with Him, I can endure it. And today, after watching that funeral tape last night, I cried so hard my eyes were soooooo puffy. All day today they were puffy and they burned – even though I had slept eight hours and it had been the afternoon of the next day. They still burned though I had cried so many hours before. That's how hard I cried – it felt better to close them than to open them, they burned so bad. But even through all my pain I can say I'm OK because of the Lord although I miss Gabe so much. I wish I felt closer to him. I wish he didn't die so long ago – then he would be more clear in my mind. I would remember him better and I would feel closer to him. I want so badly for him to be a part of my life, and for him to lead his own. I want to hear his voice again. I want to hear him laugh. I want to hang out with him. I want my big brother back. I know I can't, but watching that video made me miss him more because I remembered even more strongly what I was missing. It reminded me again of who was missing in my life. All his friends looked so young at the funeral – it scared me to see how much time had passed. He hasn't been with me in that long?! Is that right? Look how little his friends, his peers are! Look at Jake and Zack! They are so young! Was this really that long ago? All these things ran through my mind. It scared me a little – I don't want it to be that long ago – and I want the time we spent together to not be so distant. I want it to be a part of my life I can remember better. I want to remember him better. I feel like I'm experiencing all the same feelings from that day of the funeral. It was so real, I felt I was there again – if that isn't time travel, I don't know what is! I was sitting in Starbucks after I wrote all this – I so desperately wanted to see someone I knew, someone to talk to. And I did as I was leaving. I ran into Shirin, one of his and my friends from high school. We went to Hume Lake camp together and everything. We sat and talked for about an hour. It helped me get so much off my mind and we got to talk about it so much. Again, God provided that for me. I ran into her just as I was leaving after writing all of the above, just after it was closing. Only God has such right timing. Again, he continues to come through for me! I was again taken care of. I started the day with reliance and need of Him, and now I end the day with thanksgiving and appreciation to Him.

❧ October 26, 2003 ❧

I never realized how smart a 13 year-old could be; how aware and how smart. But this isn't so much about that 13 year-old as it is the whole conversation we had. We (Zack and I) were driving home from church, and he said how it was weird that Gabe dies at 17, dad's dad dies at 17, Joni Eareckson Tada was paralyzed at 17, etc. He said, "Wow, so much happens at that age," to all those people. I said, " Do you think about Gabe a lot?" (This is the first time we ever had a private conversation about this). He said, " Yes," and started to cry. So did I. I said, "What do you think about? Do you ever dream about him? Do you think about him the whole rest of the day when it gets in your mind??"… And he said yes to both, but he didn't remember the dream, but he knew he had one. Right away we opened up to each other so easily. I didn't turn on to our street to go home – I told him I was going to keep on driving. I asked him, " Do you think about how he would have been today?" and he said, " Yes." "In what way?" And he said, " I keep thinking if he were here I might be an uncle right now. There might be another little Nathan (like our little cousin)." That made my cry. I never knew he thought of it like that. I always figured he was only 9 at the time. Maybe he's trying to figure it all out. And he is, but he's beyond that. He's thinking he might have been an uncle if Gabe were here if he were married and had kids. I told him I pictured myself telling my future kids they have Uncle Jake, Uncle Zack, and an Uncle Gabe they'll meet in heaven. We talked about so much today – probably for about 3 hours we talked. He opened my eyes so much – even though I'm almost 20, and he's 13, he comforted me in such a special way. I've never talked to either of my brothers about this until today. And I've been meaning to talk to Zack about it. I wanted to know what he thought about it now – he was only 9 years old! Imagine handling something so heavy at such a young age. I asked him if he understood it – and he understood it far better than I thought. We both get bothered when someone says something like, if this or that happens, then I'll kill myself or something along those lines. When I asked him if he understood it, he said, " Yes and I hate it when people say that." He said, "I hear that every day. At school or something, someone will say it." I told him, "I know I hate it when people do that, and they don't even know. They're not even aware of it. They use it like a regular saying." He said he wished Gabe was alive so he could have met all of his new friends. I told him how it made me sad he's not around to be the first child to do everything – to take the next step in life before I did. And now I'm the one who does it first, and I've already surpassed the age he reached on earth. After talking to Zack I appreciated how well I knew him. How much time and how much of my life was with him. It hurt me so bad to hear how much in pain Zack was because he was so young when Gabe died. He doesn't remember for sure his last memory with him, and he says in the last year he barely saw him. I realized how right he was. Gabe was barely home. There's this whole other perspective that knows the pain just like I do, but in a different version, a different perspective. I told him how much Gabe loved him, and how he would always give him the front seat when he drove and all kinds of other stuff. I told him how much he reminds me of Gabe, how much he looks and acts like him. He cried so hard because he didn't know how important he was to Gabe. I told him that in many ways Gabe favored him (but there are no favorites, and we get something of value from each of our siblings). He said he never knew – why didn't anyone tell him. I felt so bad. I wanted to help him so much, but I can't go back and change how young he was, and I can't bring Gabe to him any more than I can bring Gabe to me. He said at 9 years old. He didn't really understand what was going on, but he knew his brother was dead. But he now feels deep guilt for how he felt then. He said he loved him and he missed him but he didn't have to go to school for a while. And he said it felt like it was a vacation. I feel such pain for him because he says he wishes he could have been older. He said if it were now, he could remember him so much better, and he would have felt more sad He would have cried more. He would have understood better. He said he saw Jake and my orange strings on our wrists or backpacks, and hc regrets so much that his might be in the trash somewhere. I'm crying so much as I write this because I know that pain of regret. Of wanting to hold dear something representing him but losing it or something. If he were older hc said he would have realized it was something special and he would have saved it. He regrets it now. I know exactly something like that now, because after he died I wanted to hold on to anything that belonged to him or reminded me of him. And to feel like I had something but threw it away not recognizing its importance – that would hurt so bad. Because you can never get more of those things. I cry for myself and him now. I knew he must think about him, but I never knew in that way, or what was in his mind. But at the same time he taught me so much. He expanded my mind on the topic. I was blown away to hear his perspective. It's so similar to mine, although seven years separate us – mentally, emotionally, etc. It still affected him just like it affected me. He didn't know Gabe cared about him that much. I told him things he didn't remember. I'm so glad I was able to give him more of a positive perspective. I can't believe he didn't know Gabe cared about him so much. It was obvious to me. I wish I could pass on to him some of the love and memories Gabe and I shared. I wish I could give him more. But I cannot go back and add years to their relationship. It makes me so sad to think that all of this he didn't know until today. That's what he said. He said, " I didn't know he cared about me so much." He said he thought he was just his little brother. I told him, "Nooooooo. He loved you. He loved you so much I was jealous sometimes of how well he treated you, how I thought he favored you." He said the same memories keep playing in his head over and over again and he wished he had some new ones. I can't imagine losing someone you love, but feeling like you wish you knew them better. I feel his pain so strongly. Hearing his thoughts about not knowing how special he was to Gabe, wishing he had more memories, regretting not understanding the time following his death, etc. It all made me realize that I had a lot more time with him than I thought I did. I was able to tell him so much – so much that I thought was common knowledge. I did have a lot of time and memories with Gabe. I was more thankful today. I have had so much time and memories with him that I need to cherish, and not spend too much time wishing I had even more. Look how much I had compared to others. I am so grateful now. I can't believe Zack thought he was just a little brother to Gabe. Nothing very special. He was soooooo special to Gabe. We all were but each in a different way. Just like we all have a different view of Gabe. I'm glad I got to be so close to him and talk so much to him. I'll hold on to all of those times forever; and I'm glad I have a lot to hold on to. And if anything were to happen to me, I would know that I lived and loved to the fullest. I'll still keep thinking, I'm so sad for all this time Zack didn't know how special he was to Gabe. And when I told him he reminded me so much of Gabe, he cried even more. (There were a lot of tears today). He said no one has ever told him that. He found out so much today and so did I. I'm so glad I talked to him today. I'm not going to wait so long to do it again next time. I feel so blessed to have gotten the time I did with Gabe, and so blessed to have such a strong family for support. My eyes were opened so much today by Zack's perspective. I was worried about him that one day he'd get older and realize what happened and he would feel alone. I didn't want him to feel that way. I'm so glad we talked. And I told him that and we were both thought, yeah, we never knew each other's sides to the story. I'm amazed at age 9, even then, how aware he was. He said truthfully that sometimes it feels like everyone is over it. He said I'm not. I said I'm not either. We were such a help to one another today. He didn't think that he was that close to Gabe, and I showed him that he was. I didn't think I was that close to him, but Zack showed me that I was. I'm still amazed at how he saw it, how it affected him, his feelings. I just had no idea what his feelings were. And sometimes he'll do things a certain way because it reminds him of Gabe or something they did, and it makes him feel closer to Gabe. I cried so hard when he said that because I do that too. I'll do things a certain way because it reminds me of him or a memory and it makes me feel closer to him. Oh, I cried so hard on that. I know exactly what it's like to want to feel close to Gabe, and so I do something that makes me feel closer to him, but I still miss him just as much; sometimes more. I'm just so glad we talked so we could help each other.

❧ October 27, 2003 ❧

Memories...

- When mom and dad would leave, he would make us clean up the kitchen.
- He would yell at me when I would call the dog at the same time as him and the dog would come to me.
- No game could be played without teams, points, rewards, winners and losers.
- We would watch Jerry Springer late at night (sometimes with Adam M. too).
- He bought the same Nike sandals as me for the Lake Mead houseboat trip.
- He yelled at me for getting him in a choke hold in the water – that was wrong of me. I think he was scared he couldn't breathe.
- The loud way he would eat cereal on our WA, D.C. trip.
- The spoon he kept permanently in the gallon of ice cream.
- Keeping his shoes so clean.
- Telling guys he would break their arm/neck/other body part if they hurt me; scaring off potential boyfriends.
- Calling me a "scrub" in 6th grade, a "dumb freshman" in high school.
- Calling me "little Miss Perfect" for my grades, etc.
- Sneaking the car out when he only had a permit, almost letting me drive.
- Hanging out in the backyard during my 8th grade graduation party and my Sweet 16, just in the background checking things out
- Being proud of the stuff he stole – told me he was going to become a bank robber.
- Always wanted to play Monopoly – wouldn't quit until he won.

- Told me he'd take me to a party when I was a Sophomore, not a Freshman.
- Ordered Raspberry Rage at Jamba Juice.
- Would go to Jack-in-the-Box instead of church (Sunday school).
- Told me truthfully (and amazed) how I was good at karate, was one of the best grapplers "in there". Was really amazed at how I almost beat him. Maybe I did, don't remember.
- We sparred each other really hard.
- The way he would yell at me: KATIE!!! exaggerating the two syllables.
- He would fix his hair perfect, his white shirt, jeans, big chain, all perfect.
- One time told a restaurant host how he got dressed, showered, brushed his teeth that morning – all in 5 minutes! He was so young the host just said, "Really?!" and laughed.
- Told all his teachers thank you on elementary graduation day.
- Was so polite to grandma and grandpa.
- Always was complimented on his strong handshake.
- Asked me in 7th grade why I was wearing my new pants two days in a row – I realized it was kind of weird, but he actually said something.
- Loved football.
- Could make anyone laugh.
- Put fake mice in the (elementary) principal's desk drawer on April Fools Day. (She made an announcement later).
- Was offended when I asked him if he was using his ADHD diagnosis as a crutch/scapegoat.
- Got me a present when he went to Disneyland with Brett.
- Cried when we left him at Agape.
- Would come up to me at Granada to ask for $1 for food.
- Made fun of me and my friends, but had crushes on some of them and looked out for them like he did for me.
- Would sometimes hang out with me and my friends.

- Yelled at me when I had people over when mom and dad weren't there (and they didn't know about it).
- Yelled at me for talking on the phone at 2:00am to "Mr. P".
- Called his friends to bring him over cigarettes when he was on house arrest.
- Smoked in the backyard.
- Tried to get matches to stay lit as he dropped them flame-first into a bottle.
- Sometimes so mean, sometimes so nice.
- Came to me when he was mad at mom and dad.
- Came to me when he thought he messed up his life.
- Hugged each other so tight and cried when we said good-bye when Trevor picked him up; when we didn't know where he was going.
- Sometimes talked about our weekend together.
- Would sometimes go to the mall with me but didn't want to be seen with his "little sister".
- I remember how I felt when he stopped calling me his "little sister" and started calling me his sister.
- Would ask me about this guy or that guy, making sure we were "just friends", then he'd say oh, all right.
- So protective when it came to boyfriends.
- Had a gate key to the school to get out; he was friends with the security guard.
- His high school counselor loved him, knew him out of her hundreds of students, by name.
- Would throw my clothes out of the drier to put his in.
- Would say sorry, sorry, sorry when he was caught.
- Would usually get what he wanted in the long run.
- Loved Big Macs and Coke.
- Would only bring a folder to school, but would keep all of his stuff neat; yet was ok with getting a "D" in the class.
- Would crack up so hard he couldn't breathe – we had the same laugh – and we would make each other laugh so hard going back and forth that we could barely get the words out.

- Watching The Simpson's together – he's just like Bart, me like Lisa.
- He and Trevor cracking up Sara and I on the way home on the bus from Hume Lake – talking like hicks.
- Starting and finishing a rap song the other was singing.
- He would be into some of the stuff I bought, did, etc and want to see it; vice versa to what I bought, did, etc.
- He sold me pink paper clips for $4.00 – ripped me off because I didn't know any better. Dad would tell him "No" to other such attempts – told him to wait until I learned. Told him not to give me the answers to his money counting questions, said I had to learn for myself.
- Was going to let me ride with him to school on the first day he got his car – but then told me, "No, Katie, not today, not the first day." He wanted it to be special just for him.
- People asked me about his orange Camaro, "Did your brother get a car? When? Why orange?" etc.
- Told me about people at school – people he was really close to and people he was kind of close to but they act like it's more of a relationship than is really there.
- We held each other in the cul-de-sac, shaking because of the ground beneath us in the '94 earthquake. We were barefoot and trembling.
- He loved my cats especially Buttons. "Katie, catch Buttons for me please?!" "Why don't you do it?" (But I knew the answer). "She won't come to me, she likes you." Then if I did he would keep her trapped in his room for so long. "See she likes me!" And then he'd release his grip on her body for a second, then clamp his hands back down when she would try to dash to the open bedroom door.
- Loved the Miami Dolphins.
- Loved Nike shoes.
- Gave me a new puka shell necklace at Hume Lake because he broke the one I got in Hawaii.
- White hooded sweatshirt

- Told people at Hume Lake how close and how tight we were, and how he loved me and looked out for me; how we were close in private, not in public, or how we didn't always act like it, or something like that.
- Told little punks that his sister could beat them up.
- Once asked if I would hit a girl for him because he wasn't allowed to; he was disappointed when I declined.
- He liked to stay late and play after school (elementary); I didn't.
- My parents told me he would protect me when I went from kindergarten playground to big kid" one.
- Was hard on Mike in the beginning, but then treated him really good when he realized he was a good boyfriend.
- Laughed so hard at Francis Chan's talks at camp.
- We would joke a little bit even after the talks about some of the really funny jokes.
- He started pillow fights in the middle of the night – cabin ambushing another cabin – so bad they made a camp-wide announcement saying it had to stop.
- Made me feel safe and secure and taken care of, even if he was the one teasing me. He would tease me, sometimes really bad. But if there were anything else that someone did bad to me, he wouldn't let them do it. Only he would tease me. If anyone else did, it was all over. He would fight for me, defend me till the end. We had a strong family connection.
- People would meet me and say, " You're Gabe's sister? You're so different!" I was the A-student. He was the rebel. But we both were happy. We both had a lot of friends. We both were content. Or maybe he wasn't as content as I thought.
- He picked me up from Nobel in the cul-de-sac across from the school. He was in the go-cart and my backpack dragged on the ground and got holes in it. He didn't slow down when I told him to.
- He threw us off the jet skis so many times. I wouldn't ride

with him after it threw us off and he landed on me! He laughed till he saw I was hurt then he made sure I was OK. Then he joked about throwing us off again.

- His hands were always scabbed, his knees always bruised.
- He would get me Bath and Body Works perfume for my birthday all the time, couple of years in a row. (Then was embarrassed to carry the girly bag around the mall!)
- Asked me to cover for him, help him not get in trouble.
- Kept his things very neat and clean.
- Wrote his name everywhere – on my stuff, my reminder/phone number papers, anywhere he felt like it.
- Liked a cheerleader named Andrea.
- Drove his teachers crazy, but they loved him, anyway.
- Happy, cheerful, outgoing.
- Loved to jump on my bed while I was sitting on it and lay on the covers because my bed is so comfortable.
- Would come in my room to hide when he didn't want to be found by my brothers ready to wrestle him; or my parents to remind him of some kind of work he needed to do.
- He would laugh when they discovered him, laugh when they didn't, then remind me, "Shhhhh!"
- Would jump onto my bed, get under the covers and pretend to be sleeping, snoring loudly, when I wanted him to leave. Usually he would end up staying, I would let him. He was too funny, too much of a crack up to really kick him out.
- He would encourage Jake and Zack to do the same thing. They would all be wrestling throughout my room making so much noise.
- We had such a special connection. We annoyed each other so much, but we really did look out for each other. We took care of each other because we loved each other even though we drove each other crazy. We were so opposite, yet so similar.

❧ Monday, November 17, 2003 ❧

I'm reminded of growth tonight. I watched four people get their Black Belts tied around them, after so many years of hard work. I have been fortunate to see the last few months of their training, and even from just that amount of time, I was struck with happiness and joy for them. Also, I got to work personally with the person who became a third degree Black Belt tonight (Mr. Danny Janklow). So I had a more personal interest in the candidates, especially Mr. Janklow. I was so happy for them, and I also talked to Emiko who became Mrs. Madison. That 11/15, the day of her test, was a day that I lost someone, too. She shared with me that she became a widow, lost him to cancer, four years ago. And I told her that I also lost someone, a family member, four years ago. I told her the day and she said that must have been a hard day for you. I told her I'm a Christian and I get my strength from Christ. I told her I prayed for strength to get through the day, and He gave it to me. I also said how Black Belt tests are so emotional, and that emotion added to the day – so without that strength from Christ I would have had a hard time. She liked how I wear orange on certain days. I shared with her and she said, "wow, we have a connection! That's amazing!" I was glad to share it with her. And a bit to my surprise, this four year anniversary came and went with little impact. I don't credit that to a lack of pain, or myself moving on. I credit that to Christ's amazing way of providing for me and giving me strength. I needed His strength to persevere through that day. And looking back, I asked God if it were possible to handle the pain, deal with the pain, early. I was asking of it would be possible, if I could please do that if possible. I wanted to "finish the job" and let the pain hit me before the testing day. I knew I would need to focus and be alert on that day. I wouldn't be able to be Mr. Janklow's partner and be giving, and expect to think of myself at the same time. So now I realized that I handled the pain early. I didn't know emotions could be handled so objectively, but apparently they can. So looking back at recent entries in this book, I see that I thought a lot about it before the anniversary. So I was grateful to be able to have my focus that day, because I handled the pain early, before the anniversary day. I wore an orange shirt and an orange scrunchie in my hair. I had him on my mind, but the Red and Black Belt test took precedence. I was so glad. But on the other hand, I wished I could just take my time out to remember him. I was a little disappointed the test was on November 15th. I was disappointed. I even needed to pray for strength that day. I thought he must not be very important to me that I can brush aside such an important day so easily. But I really wanted to be there to watch the students testing. I wanted to be there for them. I'm not focusing very well right now – I'm listening to Christmas music and zoning out. Basically, this four year anniversary hit me before the actual day, due to my prayer request; and Him fulfilling yet another one of my requests. He humbles me with how good and how generous He is with me. And I told both Mr. And Mrs. Ercolono that I am so grateful for being a part of their school. This was some time after he gave me a hug and said thank you for being a part of his school and bringing energy to his students. And I was so thankful for that, and I feel so appreciative for how much he has given to me. The respect, I told them, is so amazing, and I never saw karate through their perspective, that peaceful perspective. I told them thank you so much, and how I wish I could have been there years ago, and how I wish I could be there for years to come. But he said to just enjoy it for what it is. He said, "That's what I'm going to do." And it was so nice. And Mrs. Ercolono said she loves how the students say, "Yes, ma'am!", when she asks them to do something. She was thinking, I'm so glad Miss Williams is having them do this! I was glad to hear it. I'm just so glad to be there. I'm going to take so much from The Way. I'm so, so, so fortunate to be there for as long as I get to be. And in the process I have learned more about myself, my life, and how I want it to be. Also, I have learned through Mr. Ercolono about strength, choices, and how both of these can influence us for the better; influence our lives for the better. I have learned so much from him in the past few months I've been at The Way. I have learned things that I know I will always carry with me. Not things about karate, but about life. Although he has taught me many things about karate, too, it's the other stuff that's really valuable to me. It's those things that have such an influence on me. I'll definitely take them with me to my last years of college and beyond. And maybe one day I'll share with him what happened with me losing Gabe, if the opportunity presents itself, or if I just want to tell him. Until then, I just love karate, and The Way and the Ercolono's! Josh told me he's really happy for me, glad that I love the karate studio so much. He said the more I talk about it, with time, the better it sounds. Yes, he's right.

Afterthought: (1/11/04)

That night I was so excited and filled with a joy that normally would have been so inappropriate on this anniversary, considering my feelings. But I was happy and talking to everyone, filled with a joy that is so high I don't often feel something of such a magnitude. I truly felt His strength was made perfect in my weakness.

Hillsdale Essay

It was not what I expected, nor what I wanted; but it happened. It was a cold Monday night in November, well as cold as it gets in southern California, and I was in my usual routine. I was at the karate studio, something I did three times a week. My karate instructor approached me on the mat during class and told me that my mom was on the phone. Well, its not the kind of distraction I wanted at this time, at this place where I come to focus my body and mind. But it's my mom, so of course I pick up the phone. "Hi mom." "Hi honey, I'm not going to pick you up tonight, Tom the neighbor will." "OK mom. But why, what happened? Did they find Gabe yet?" Her phone cut out. I never heard her answer. But now in hindsight, I think she chose to hang up on me – I would find out later why she chose to do that. I asked her about Gabe, my older brother who had ran away from home the night before. The police were involved and looking for him, and this was not the first time they had gone looking for him. But I figured everything would be fine, the police would find him, and he would be in trouble – again. I was used to this by now, my 17 year old brother getting into trouble and giving my parents more than a handful to deal with. So karate class ended, and like my mom had told me, our neighbor came and picked me up.

We drove toward my neighborhood, not a very far distance from the karate studio, passing under only a few green lights as we went. But to my surprise we didn't go to my house, nor Tom's house. We went to my aunt and uncle's house, just a few blocks away in the same area. I knew I was missing something and I was very confused. We turned on to their street and for a moment, I thought I saw something... I looked again. There were several cop cars parked on the opposite side of the street from my uncle's house. The odd thing was they were laying flares down on the street in a kind of semi-circle blocking it off. And just for a brief moment I thought to myself, "Could those be for Gabe?" "No," I reassured myself, they wouldn't go to all that work for a runaway kid. I had just turned 16 at the time, and I wished I had already gotten my license so I could drive across the street myself and see what the flares were for. But I couldn't, so instead I thanked Tom for the ride and I went inside. My two younger brothers were already there. More confusion. "Why are we all here?" "Where are my parents?" "What's really going on?" "Why wasn't my mom able to pick me up from karate?" Those questions would have to wait because my brothers and my cousins were about to watch "The Matrix". How ironic. I knew something was going on, but trying to keep a level head, I sat and watched the movie. Somewhere in between the time after Neo had taken the pill, and Morphous had tried to defeat the enemy, there was a knock at the door. It was my parents. I just have to interject here for a moment and say I'm very close to my family. I thought I had seen all sides of each member of my immediate family. But to say that before this night would have been a lie. I have never seen my dad's face like this. He looked like he had aged a matter of seven years in one night. Everyone came into the living room when they came through the door. My brothers and I were on the couch, my parents seated themselves on the rug beneath us, and the others stood behind the couch patiently. I knew I was out of the loop on something and I feared it. I thought, "OK, here comes the news. Gabe will be back in juvenile hall, kiddy jail, and when he comes out we'll all have more house rules to follow just like last time." I was wrong. I'll never forget the words out of my dad's mouth: "Gabe took his life tonight."

Did I hear that right? This was some "Matrix" after all. This cannot be reality. So I repeated the words out loud that were running, no racing, through my head. "No, no, no, no..." I felt if I said it enough, they would admit it wasn't true. But it was true. My big brother, my friend, the person I assumed would always would always be a part of my life was gone. I felt denial immediately while my younger brothers started to cry. Somehow I thought I could reverse it, but I knew I couldn't and I never felt so powerless. I felt so empty, so alone, like all my insides had been ripped out and I would need major surgery. This is how weak and impaired I felt. I didn't want to cry, because if I cried that would be acknowledging that it was true. And I kept thinking I could do something, could make my brother come back, and could undo this horrible night's events.

In the days, weeks, and now almost four years that have passed since that painful night, I have grown in ways that I never thought possible. There were so many people that came to my family and my aid – it was amazing. Gabe was such a popular guy – there were so many people at the funeral and at my house in the time that followed. And I missed him – bad. My heart had never known so much pain, and I wasn't quite sure what to do with it all. I had a desperate desire to see him, talk to him again. I felt expectant for a long time that he was going to come walking in through the front door. But he never did. We were close and I felt his absence strongly. Sure we hated each other at times – we are siblings after all! But we always had a special closeness, a relationship that only us two together could bring about the right chemistry to create. And I miss that, and I miss him to this day, even in this moment while I write. I can still see his face. Blond hair with baby blues and a smile that could win him just about anything he wanted except an answer to his pain! Pain that I didn't know was so strong within him. But now this pain in me, mourning, brings about great growth.

Of course immediately after he died I wondered, "What happens next?" Well, that is the ultimate question, isn't it? It's the one I sometimes ask myself over and over to reassess where I am in my life and in my healing process. This experience has had more of an impact on me than any other. Every day it affects me differently; sometimes it inspires me, sometimes it discourages me. It continues to push me and make me grow, and it forces me to handle loads I never thought I could. And I can't handle these loads, not alone. Just so the reader knows, 'can't' isn't a word I use lightly. In fact, I never use it because I don't want to shorten my sights for myself or doubt that I can do something. So 'can't' is not in my dictionary. But this unexpected work load, this struggling and mourning the loss of my brother and missing him; this is what has caused me growth. Growth as a person, and more importantly growth in and with Christ. This experience has done the most valuable things for me, even amidst all the pain. It has brought me closer in the direction of my Lord. Before Gabe died, I went to church every week, I tithed, and I would pray sometimes. Mostly just when I needed something or when I was scared. I did those things because I was taught this way, but I had not adopted these ways for myself. But once Gabe died I felt a weight that even my optimistic attitude and my perseverance could not handle. I felt so many times that I couldn't do it. And it's true I really couldn't do it. And so for the first time, I could not rely on my own strength to pull me through. I remember that first honest prayer, that time when I came to the Lord, broken and unable to handle the pain myself. I was looking for help, and He gave me the peace that surpasses all understanding. The kind I had heard about but had never experienced. And it was the beginning of a beautiful, loving relationship. The kind of relationship where I have chosen not to fight alone, and instead rely on Him for what I need. Whether it's help with my hurting heart, the need to be comforted, given strength, or any other needs that may arise. I know He's there. And because I have chosen to rely on Christ every day for my needs, particularly the emotional needs, I know what the rest of my life will be like. I don't know for certain where I'll go or what I'll do, but I do know one thing for sure – He's with me, and that's all the security I need.

❧ November 19, 2003 ❧

I miss him a lot. I have been thinking about him so much and thinking of nothing but him and his absence. I've been hiding those true feelings behind keeping busy. I'm scared to face it. I thought I have seen the worst, but maybe there's more to come. Maybe it does get worse from here, maybe it does get worse in certain areas, in ways I haven't seen yet. I'm scared to see it. I miss him so much but I can't let it control my days. But by resisting maybe I'm making it worse in the long run. I don't know what to think or what to do now. Where do I go from here? Is the majority of my mourning over? The pain has been more intense than I thought possible, so it must subside from here, right? What do I think? What do I do? I know I feel it. I know I'm thinking about him, but should I just get used to it and whatever happens so be it? Am I going to go through another transformation, another self realization and growth period? I'm unsure. All I know is that I don't care about anything else but this right now. And am I allowed to take time off, time out of my schedule to reflect on it? No, because the show must go on. My obligations/responsibilities persist and so must I. This sucks. I have the worst, heaviest, painful feelings in my heart and I can't even nurse them. This is the most important need of my heart and I cannot even address it. My one o'clock class is in ten minutes, and again, I'm pulled back into my schedule. Yet here I am, writing about it, taking time to address it. But it's not enough time. It's never enough time! I will need so much time to feel and to fill such a void. Who could possibly fill the Grand Canyon up in just a few hours? And likewise, how could I fill the vast void in my heart in just four years time? The longing for him is so great, but there's no action I can take to fix it. I can only be comforted through Christ, through prayer. But I am disappointed because I have finally realized the void will never be filled. It will only be smoothed over on the edges, but never filled.

12th Grade written on:

❦ December 29, 2003 ❦

I got up, dressed, brushed my teeth, washed my face, and finished getting ready for school. After one last glance in the mirror I went to grab my keys and go out into the kitchen where I would eat, then leave. But I couldn't find my keys. I looked on top of my stereo next to my phone charger where I always left them, but they weren't there. Neither were they in my bedroom or bathroom, after my search of five frantic minutes, overturning even that dirty pain of jeans I wore last week. I hurried to the kitchen, explaining the situation to my dad. He concluded that I would have to take the family van to school – great just what I love, "the van". I head back to my room for one last look for my keys because I'm desperate. I pray I will find them. I pray God will show me: please, where they are? I hear, or feel the words, "You'll have them before you go to school." Thinking that the words were my own, just words I was feeding to myself, I disregarded them and left my room. I drove the van and met my dad for coffee at a place nearby school, about a half an hour before school would start. We sat, my dad, brother and I, drinking our coffee, enjoying the morning before my dad would go to work, and Jake and I would go to school. I remembered the words I had heard in my bedroom, but I, again, didn't really believe them or place much weight on them because I thought the task was impossible. I thought I was mixing my words and God's words, telling myself what I wanted to hear, yet confused about whether or not I had thought the words. As we left the coffee house and we were walking out into the parking lot, my dad reached into his jacket pocket and pulled out my car keys. And out of his own pants pocket, his own car keys. I couldn't believe it; I had got my car keys before I went to school. It was absolutely amazing and I couldn't rationalize it. What God said had come true, and I could not explain it any other way than God doing exactly what He said He was going to do. It felt like a miracle. I couldn't explain it, but God did. In fact, He explained it before it happened. I didn't tell my dad then just how amazed I was that he pulled my keys out of his own jacket pocket. On the surface, it seemed, my dad remembered that he borrowed my car, or I borrowed his jacket. We never did quite figure it out. But God was right; He said it would happen and it did. I was ashamed that I didn't believe Him the first time He said it, but I was relieved that He was right, that it was in His hands the whole time. He just chose to let me in on a little secret. I just needed to believe it when He whispered it to me. I felt so stupid for not believing Him. Who am I to question God who sees everything?

10th Grade

❧ January 11, 2004 ❧

I was just about to leave for school, and I took one last look into my room to make sure I hadn't forgotten anything I needed to bring. I walked to the side of my bed and looked down at my Bible on the nightstand. I felt a tugging at my heart to bring my Bible to school. I felt like God was telling me to bring it. And then my intellectual side, the side that wants to reason and rationalize everything kicked on. Then I was having an internal struggle wondering why I should bring my Bible to school. I went through my six periods, wondering which class I would use it in. None. And so I ignored God's words to my heart, telling me to bring my Bible to school. I'm not going to use it in any of my classes, why should I bring it? That day I walked with Mike to his locker during lunchtime so he could get his food. This was a routine we did about two or three times a week, a typical pattern. But this day was different. I looked through the open classroom door right next to his locker, and I saw a group of people meeting inside. Two students were at the front of the room, and the rest of the people were seated, listening with their Bibles open on their desks. It was a Bible study! I had never seen this before, and I didn't know there was such a meeting, even though Mike and I walked right past this room dozens of times before this! It was amazing – I just couldn't believe what had happened. God was telling me to bring my Bible to school knowing I was going to be attending a Bible study that day. I just had no idea; I should have had blind faith and brought it to school, despite my doubts. Mike and I are both Christians, and when we saw what it was we went in for the remainder of the time. Also, the two students giving the talk were our friends, Danny and Will. Will I knew from church, Danny he knew from basketball. Imagine, that whole time, how close we were to the room, even knowing both of the leaders, but never knowing it was there. And then when God asked me to trust Him with something so simple, just carrying an extra book to school, I didn't. Well, I've learned my lesson, and I'm glad he taught me. He knew what was in store that day, I just needed to trust Him.

Final Thoughts

⎯ ∞ ⎯

That is the story of me losing my brother, and how God changed that negative into a positive. However, there is something left to be said. What Gabe did was wrong. He had no right to take something that didn't belong to him; but he did anyway and God used that unfortunate and sad event to touch many people, in the way I hoped that it touched you. I also want to offer hope to people that struggle with suicide. There are solutions to problems, and suicide is not a solution to any problem or any pain. There are many support groups, crises hotlines, and other groups that reach out to those who struggle with suicide. To truly understand this problem and to help prevent it there are some warning signs and things to be aware of:

- Suicidal threats. (Take these seriously. Even if the person has only mentioned it once. These kinds of thoughts come at times of extreme depression usually. And even when the depression lifts, that doesn't mean the risk of that person committing suicide lifts – especially for the first few months afterward. Sometimes, a person may seem peaceful because they have found an 'answer' to their problems, meaning they have decided to take their life.)
- Suicide attempts.
- Statements about feeling depressed, hopeless, worthless, unhappy, anxious, upset, sluggish, or moody.
- Preoccupation with death.
- Loss of interest in hobbies or activities they previously enjoyed.

- The giving away of personal items.
- Use of alcohol.
- Visiting and calling people they care about; setting their affairs in order.

   Not all people with depression or suicidal thoughts will show them in the same way. The important thing to do is get a suicidal person professional help – a doctor or psychiatrist who knows how to handle the situation. Suicide is not the answer. There is help and there is always hope.

Additional Sources and References: Helpful Books, Phone Numbers, and Websites

- *Shattered Dreams: God's Unexpected Pathway to Joy* by Larry Crabb
- *When God Weeps: Why Our Sufferings Matter to the Almighty* by Steven Estes and Joni Eareckson Tada
- *Letter to a Grieving Heart* by Billy Sprague
- *His Bright Light* by Danielle Steel
- *A Decembered Grief* by Harold Ivan Smith
- *Lament for a Son* by Nicholas Wolterstorff
- *The Bible*

- 1-800-SUICIDE, a hotline for those who are seeking hope and who find trained counselors to speak to 24 hours a day, 7 days a week

- www.save.org, the website of Suicide Awareness Voices of Education
- www.survivorsofsuicide.com, a site designed to help those who have lost a loved one to suicide
- www.yellowribbon.org, a site educating and promoting suicide prevention among teens
- www.suicidology.org, the website of the American Association of Sociology whose purpose is to promote prevention and an understanding of suicidal people

About the Author

Katie Williams was born in Mission Hills, a quiet suburb of Los Angeles, California. She lived there until age six when her family moved to another suburban area not far away, Northridge. This is where she lived with her parents Allen and Chris, and her older brother Gabe, and younger brothers, Jake and Zack. She attended local public schools for elementary, junior high, and high school. This quiet area is classified as a typical middle class neighborhood, like many others in America. Her upbringing is best described as a family oriented, and fun loving. Williams was involved in many activities both in and out of school, throughout the years from elementary to high school. Some of those activities include holding offices in student council, playing on soccer teams at a local park, going to church with her family, snowboarding in the mountains not far from home, and studying the martial arts. Martial arts played a large role in Williams's activities growing up, beginning in the sixth grade, and continuing through college. It has been the dominant activity of her life thus far. In the winter of 1999 with the suicide of her seventeen-year-old brother Gabe, she began to acquaint herself with a new world that no longer included her brother. She wrote down her private thoughts in a journal about her emotions, questions, and method of coping while grieving this loss. She is currently studying Speech Communications at a small private college in Hillsdale, Michigan. *Journey of the Heart: Transforming the Tragedy of a Family Suicide into Healing, Beauty, and Discovering God* is her first published work, and her hope for her journal is that it will help others understand and survive the pain of losing a loved one. Her future goals are to become a successful author and public speaker.

A handwritten 8.5 x 11" version of Katie Williams "Journey of the Heart" is also available at her website: www.livingwaterpub.com. See a sample page below (half size):

⁓ other forms of what you thought you used to have; they only skim the surface, & it is a cheap imitation. Nothing else will satisfy such a deep hunger. That's what makes it so difficult sometimes. When my ♡ hurts, & I miss him, I realize that my ♡ is going through something so deep, so hurtful, that nothing else going on around me is as important. It requires my immediate attention. That is when the glasses come on, & I see what's really important. food & air are second to it. It's that deep. People who haven't felt that kind of depth don't really understand how important it is to nurse the wounds when they re-open. That's what sets me apart from ppl. I'm talking life & death, they're talking chinese or Mexican for lunch. No comparison. The good thing though is that it grounds you. When I get caught up in my life, & I see something & I get a little remembrance of him I again am grounded & reminded of what is really important. then I'm glad I'm spending time w/ friends & other important ppl to me. His death has added so much meaning & understanding. Rather, it revealed to me how important the ppl, not things, are in my life. I feel such deep pain, but that reflects how much, deep love I had for him that almost 4 yrs later I still miss him this much. Hit me like a wave today. I was missing him so much. Confused @ what happened & why it did. Reflecting on how fast it all happened. After the many, many tears, I felt comforted. Because I prayed but also because if I "hurt this much, it's because I loved him that much. His former presence was so significant that even after 4' this time his absence is still noted. That did give me some comfort. I still wish so much that he was here. I expected him to be here today & everyday & I took it for granted. I miss

- 127 -